a paella pan on every
backyard grill in America.

made in spain

andalucía
madrid
país vasco
navarra
cantabria
extremadura
valencia
murcia
galicia
cataluña
castilla y león
aragón
asturias
castilla la mancha
la rioja
baleares
canarias

made in spain

Spanish Dishes for the American Kitchen

José Andrés
with Richard Wolffe

Food photographs by
Thomas Schauer

Clarkson Potter / Publishers
New York

Published in the United States by Clarkson Potter/Publishers, an imprint of the Crown Publishing Group, a division of Random House, Inc., New York.

www.crownpublishing.com
www.clarksonpotter.com

Clarkson Potter is a trademark and Potter with colophon is a registered trademark of Random House, Inc.

Library of Congress Cataloging-in-Publication Data
Andrés, José.
Made in Spain : Spanish dishes for the American kitchen / José Andrés.—1st ed.
p. cm.
1. Cookery, Spanish. I. Title.
TX723.5.S7A6175 2008
641.5946—dc22 2008027709

ISBN 978-0-307-38263-4

Printed in the United States of America

Art Direction / Design
by Tasty Concepts / Roberto Sablayrolles

Spain photography by Pablo de Loy.
Additional Spain photography courtesy of Tourist Office of Spain and Javier Canovas.

10 9 8 7 6 5 4 3 2 1

First Edition

To Tichi,
Carlota,
Inés,
and
Lucía

Thank you
for helping
me achieve
everything
I dream. . . .

. . . and to
the people
of Spain,
especially those
who help
tell the story
of Spain
to the world.

Contenidos

contents

Introducción

introduction

I have always dreamed of the United States. As a child, I was fascinated by Disney, and by the time I was a teenager, I devoured all things American. I loved movies like *Indiana Jones* and *Star Wars* and would stay up until 4:00 in the morning to watch Magic Johnson and Larry Bird play in the NBA finals. My first visit to the States came while serving as a crew member on a Spanish navy ship—a 1920s tall ship called the *Juan Sebastían Elcano* after the great sixteenth-century explorer. We docked in Pensacola, Florida, which was like a dream to me because it was founded by a Spanish conquistador. Pensacola is known as the city of five flags for the five nations that ruled it in turn: Spain, France, Britain, the Confederacy, and the United States. There I befriended the owner of a local restaurant and wondered when I would return. By the time we reached our next port of call, New York, my mind was made up. At the time, I was the skinniest, fastest man on board, and I had the best post—at the top of the tallest mast. Sailing into New York Harbor, I was overcome by the sight of the Statue of Liberty. I knew I'd find my way back.

After leaving the navy, I started my career in Spain as a chef. I didn't think too much more about my dream of coming to the United States until I heard of a wonderful opportunity. It was 1991, just before the Barcelona Olympics, and there was a lot of American interest in Catalonian restaurants. A new one was opening in New York, and I jumped at the chance to work there. Sadly, the restaurant, Paradis Barcelona, didn't succeed. But I soon heard of another restaurant, El Dorado Petit, opening in a few months—a spinoff of a Barcelona institution that was one of the top three restaurants in the world. El Dorado Petit was a great fit for me because I had just spent time working with Ferran Adrià at El Bulli, widely recognized as the best, most creative restaurant in the world today.

Now I had a new dream: to bring Spanish food to the United States. Today, many people tell me I'm a visionary for knowing that Spanish cooking was going to become as successful and popular as it has become. But I can only look back and smile. I didn't choose to focus on Spanish cooking; it was the only thing I knew.

But what exactly *is* Spanish cooking? When I first arrived in the States, my idea of Spanish gastronomy was different from the food I have come to cook at my tapas restaurants. As a young chef, I was even a little bit ashamed of traditional Spanish cooking. Although I knew a lot about traditional food, my background was in Michelin-starred restaurants like El Bulli, where the focus was on creative cooking. To us, tapas were something to eat when we didn't have much money. It took me four or five years in the United States to figure out it doesn't matter if Spanish cooking is modern or traditional; it's all Spanish, and it's all worth fighting for. I realized that tapas—at the high or low end—were the single best way to bring Spanish food to the States.

The revelation started with some wise advice from one of my first mentors: Clemente Bocos, an important figure in Spanish cooking in America. Clemente owned a tiny tapas bar called El Cid in downtown Manhattan. He and his wife, Yolanda, were like family, and they took care of me. At the time, my restaurant, El Dorado Petit, didn't have any clarity of direction, and it kept changing recipes. In the end, they didn't resemble what they were back home in Barcelona. My friend Clemente said, "José, you know very well how to cook. You need to follow your instincts. Don't Americanize anything. You need to cook for yourself and to please yourself. It's the only way you'll be able to please others and make sure they enjoy your cooking and Spanish cooking."

It was that spirit that helped make my Jaleo restaurants so successful in the Washington, D.C., area: an authenticity based on real Spanish ingredients and uncomplicated Spanish cooking. That was also the inspiration for my public television show, *Made in Spain.* I wanted to show U.S. viewers that they too could easily cook Spanish dishes at home, using simple American ingredients and genuine Spanish products readily bought here. Moreover, I wanted to show where all that great Spanish food and drink came from: the spirit, the people, and the land that gave birth to my cooking.

To outsiders, Spain looks like a single country, but to Spaniards, their country is a fascinating mixture of people, language, culture, and food. The regional differences across Spain reflect their contrasting geographies, climates, and histories, and those differences make for an exceptionally varied approach to what I love best: cooking and eating. If there's one thing all Spaniards share, it's a love of food and drink. From the residential markets of Madrid to the avant-garde restaurants of Catalonia, there's a deep appreciation of the highest-quality ingredients, great old traditions, and brand-new ideas—not to mention a great deal of national pride.

In this book you can find all the recipes I cook in *Made in Spain,* as well as many more dishes like those I eat on the street, at the beach, or in Spain's great restaurants. You'll also find special pages on each of the regions I visit in the show. Yet the regions are less important than the food, which is why this book is organized by the kind of dishes I think you'll want to cook.

Spain is home to some of the best ingredients in the world; our olive oil, tuna, rice, and wines are, in my opinion, unrivaled. The good news is that you can now buy them anywhere in the United States—at your local supermarket, at gourmet stores, and on the Internet. Moreover, you can cook most of the dishes in this book with the wonderful produce that grows in America and the great fish and seafood of the Pacific and Atlantic. The dishes are born in Spain, but you can make them right here in the States.

These are recipes you can make at home for family, friends, or yourself. Most of them are quick and require no special cooking techniques or equipment. All you need is your own sense of taste and an appetite to savor the flavors of Spain. I hope you *will* travel to my country in the very near future; until then, it is my wish that these recipes will whet your appetite for the best that Spain has to offer.

Everyone who knows me understands that my chauvinism for everything Spanish is so excessive that it borders on a joke. But I keep pushing to bring more of our amazing Spanish ingredients to this country. Fifteen years ago, you could count on one hand the Spanish chefs in the United States. Today there are many—and many more are coming. Back then, a number of restaurants that were cooking Spanish dishes were doing a very bad job. Today, many Spanish restaurants in many cities are doing a top job. Of course, I won't be happy until every single American backyard has a paella, not a barbecue, cooking on top of the grill on a Sunday afternoon. That's my way of measuring success fifty years from now. And I'm not joking.

QUESOS DE SIERRA DE GATA
QUESO CURADO DE CABRA
La Rozag

Between the Mediterranean sun, the great vegetable gardens of the north, and our tapas culture, Spain became a country of salads. The variety and creativity of these dishes is extraordinary, and the philosophy is unusual; few of them are the lettuce-based jumbles beloved by our European friends. What we excel at are refreshing combinations that showcase vegetables and other ingredients, such as potatoes and fish or tomatoes and cheese. Some simply pay homage to a great, fresh vegetable worth savoring in all its unadorned glory. In the great Andalusian city of Seville, where the tapas culture is an evening ritual, they might call their salads aliños, referring to the dressing on the vegetables. Or they might serve you a classic pipirrana salad of pepper, tomatoes, cucumber, and tuna. Whatever you call them, the recipes that follow can be adapted to your taste, to the season, and to whatever you have at hand—just as they are in Spain.

salads

andalucía

To many foreigners, Andalusia *is* Spain. It's the largest region in the country, with mountains, valleys, and a coastline on two seas that tourists adore. Its cities of Seville, Granada, and Córdoba are striking combinations of history and modernity, Catholicism and Islam. And its rich culture of food, wine, and fiestas is as old as it is irresistible. The Phoenicians brought vines, the Carthaginians planted garbanzos, the Romans cultivated olives, and the Arabs irrigated the land for vegetables. From its fried fish and seafood to its egg-based pastries and desserts, Andalusia is a feast.

To many Spaniards, however, Andalusia seems a bit like another country. In Spain, I'm considered a northerner because I was born in Asturias. We Asturians pride ourselves on being the *real* Spaniards, as we started the reconquest of Spain from the Moors. So to me, as a child growing up in the north, Andalusia, at the southern tip of Spain, seemed as remote as another planet. Andalusíans spoke with a different accent and were seemingly ready to sing, dance, and drink at any time.

I first visited Andalusia when I was in the navy. We sailed into Cádiz, and I can honestly say I fell in love with the region, as so many others did before me, from John Singer Sargent to Washington Irving. It's easy to understand why. People in Andalusia say there is something called *duende*, a magical spirit that inspires their culture, especially their uniquely witty sense of humor. In Andalusia, I learned to love eating at bars, even in fancy restaurants. The region also gave me a deep appreciation for the art of frying, thanks to its extraordinary *pescaito frito,* or fried fish. That dish alone is proof that the frying culture of southern Spain is more refined than any other in the world, although it remains underappreciated outside of Spain.

Andalusia is where the sun and the *duende* shine like nowhere else in the world. Maybe it was the *duende* that struck me when I first saw Patricia, the Andalusian woman who would become my wife (though she had no idea of this destiny at the time). She was dancing in my Washington restaurant, Café Atlántico, and her gestures, her smile, her accent—they were *so* Andalusian. I was instantly smitten. Now she and I, along with our children, return each summer to a small Andalusían town called Zahara de los Atúnes (literally, Zahara of the Tunas), where Europe meets Africa and the Mediterranean meets the Atlantic. As the name suggests, this is where the majestic fish migrate each year from the Arctic Circle to their mating waters in the Mediterranean. Here the tuna catch still takes place early each summer, just as it has since ancient times, using the intricate almadraba system of netting first developed by the Arabs. A little up the coast, close to Jerez and Sanlúcar de Barrameda, is sherry country, where small changes in climate can lead to big contrasts in the color and flavor of the wine. To me, a glass of great sherry is almost as refreshing as one of the salads or cold soups the region is famous for.

MANZANILL
VICTORIA

Clementinas con Chinchón, anchoas y aceitunas negras

Clementines with Chinchón, anchovy, and black olives

SERVES 4

FOR THE DRESSING

- 1 CUP SPANISH EXTRA-VIRGIN OLIVE OIL
- ¼ CUP SHERRY VINEGAR
- 4 TABLESPOONS CHINCHÓN (SPANISH ANISE-FLAVORED LIQUEUR) OR OTHER ANISETTE
- ZEST AND JUICE OF 2 CLEMENTINES
- 1 SHALLOT, THINLY SLICED
- 12 EMPELTRE OLIVES OR OTHER GOOD-QUALITY BLACK OLIVES
- SEA SALT TO TASTE

FOR THE SALAD

- ½ HEAD ROMAINE LETTUCE, TOUGH OUTER LEAVES DISCARDED
- ½ HEAD BIBB LETTUCE, TOUGH OUTER LEAVES DISCARDED
- ½ HEAD RED LEAF LETTUCE, TOUGH OUTER LEAVES DISCARDED
- 8 OIL-PACKED ANCHOVY FILLETS
- 4 CLEMENTINES, PEELED AND SLICED INTO ¼-INCH ROUNDS
- TENDER WATERCRESS LEAVES (OPTIONAL)
- SEA SALT TO TASTE

José's Tip:
If you can't find Chinchón, try another anise-flavored liqueur like Marie Brizard. If you don't have watercress for the garnish, use a little flat-leaf parsley.

Prepare the dressing: Whisk together the olive oil, vinegar, Chinchón, clementine zest and juice, shallot, and olives in a medium bowl. Season with salt and set aside.

Separate the heads of lettuce into individual leaves and divide them among 4 plates or bowls. Top each salad with 2 anchovy fillets and one-quarter of the clementine slices. Drizzle each salad with dressing, and garnish with watercress, if you like. Season to taste with salt.

Clementines are from the Mediterranean. Chinchón liqueur is from the heart of Spain. Anchovies come from Cantabria in the north. And black olives come from beautiful, sunny Andalusia. Geographically, they would never be found together, but in this salad, they exist together in perfect harmony. The striking flavor comes from the anise-flavored liqueur. If you like fennel in your salads, you'll love this dressing.

Ensaladilla rusa con huevas de trucha

Classic potato salad with crunchy trout roe

SERVES 4

FOR THE MAYONNAISE

2 LARGE EGGS

1 CUP SPANISH EXTRA-VIRGIN OLIVE OIL

1 TEASPOON FRESH LEMON JUICE

1 TEASPOON SALT

1 CUP VEGETABLE OIL

FOR THE SALAD

4 RUSSET POTATOES, PEELED

1 LARGE CARROT, TRIMMED AND PEELED

7 LARGE EGGS

16 OUNCES SPANISH CANNED TUNA, PREFERABLY OIL-PACKED BONITO, SEPARATED INTO FLAKES

1 CUP FRESH PEAS, BLANCHED (OR THAWED FROZEN PEAS)

SEA SALT TO TASTE

4 OUNCES TROUT ROE, PREFERABLY SPANISH

SPANISH EXTRA-VIRGIN OLIVE OIL

Prepare the mayonnaise: Break the eggs into a small mixing bowl and add 2 tablespoons of the olive oil, the lemon juice, and the salt. Using a hand-held electric mixer, mix at high speed, and then slowly drizzle in the remaining olive oil and the vegetable oil until you have a thick, creamy sauce.

Prepare the salad: Boil the potatoes and carrot until very soft, about 30 minutes. Drain and set aside to cool. Meanwhile, place the eggs in a saucepan with water to cover and bring to a boil. Boil the eggs for 10 minutes, drain them, and place them in a bowl of ice water to cool. Peel the eggs and cut them into 1-inch cubes. Put the chopped eggs into a large mixing bowl and add the tuna.

Cut the cooled potatoes and carrot into 1-inch cubes and add them to the tuna along with the peas. Gently stir in 1 cup of the mayonnaise, being careful not to mash the potatoes, carrot, or tuna. Season to taste with salt. (The remaining mayonnaise may be kept in the refrigerator, tightly covered, for 2 to 3 days.)

To serve, divide the salad among 4 plates and top each serving with a spoonful of trout roe. Sprinkle with salt and drizzle with olive oil.

José's Tip:
To really bring out the flavors, allow the salad to rest for 1 hour and serve at room temperature. If you can't find trout roe, use salmon roe.

This tapa is found everywhere in Spain, both in professional kitchens and on family tables. Home cooks are just as proud of their own versions as are the tapas bar owners who make it for their paying customers. At the high end, creative restaurants draw inspiration from this humble dish, dreaming up more modern interpretations. I use the great trout roe Spanish producers are now selling in the United States to lift the simple salad, adding a crunchy texture and subtle flavor to the soft potatoes and meaty tuna.

Ensalada agridulce de tomates con queso Afuega'l Pitu

Sweet-and-sour salad with tomatoes and Afuega'l Pitu cheese

SERVES 4

FOR THE DRESSING

1 TABLESPOON SPANISH CIDER VINEGAR OR A GOOD-QUALITY CIDER VINEGAR

3 TABLESPOONS SPANISH EXTRA-VIRGIN OLIVE OIL

LEAVES FROM 1 FRESH THYME SPRIG

1 TABLESPOON HONEY

SALT TO TASTE

FOR THE SALAD

8 PLUM TOMATOES

2 HEADS OF FRISÉE LETTUCE, LEAVES SEPARATED

12 CHERRY TOMATOES, HALVED

5 OUNCES AFUEGA'L PITU (SPANISH COW'S-MILK CHEESE FROM ASTURIAS)

FRESH CHERVIL SPRIGS

SEA SALT TO TASTE

José's Tip:

If you can't find the Afuega'l Pitu cheese, look for a cured cow's-milk cheese instead. Also, don't fret about the tomatoes. You can use any tomato of your choice. Just be careful with the seed fillets—they are a bit of extra work, but they look like tomato caviar. And they turn a humble salad into a special dish.

Prepare the dressing: Whisk the vinegar, olive oil, thyme leaves, and honey together in a small bowl. Season to taste with salt and set aside.

Prepare the salad: Using a sharp knife, slice off the top and bottom of each plum tomato. Find the fleshy dividing wall of one segment inside the tomato. Slice alongside the dividing wall and open the flesh of the tomato to expose the seeds. Remove the seeds and their pulp by slicing around the core of the tomato. Set the seed sacs aside. Your aim is to keep the seeds and their surrounding gel intact to create tomato seed "fillets" that are separate from the firmer tomato flesh. You should have about 16 fillets. Dice the tomato flesh and set aside.

In a large mixing bowl, toss the frisée and cherry tomatoes with 4 tablespoons of the dressing. Arrange the tomato seed fillets and diced tomato pieces on each of 4 plates. Divide the frisée and cherry tomatoes among the plates. Crumble the cheese over the greens and lay a couple chervil sprigs on top. Drizzle with a little more dressing and garnish with sea salt, if you like.

Sweet and salty is a typically Spanish combination of flavors, and our gastronomy has many examples: jamón Serrano with melon, anchovies with tomatoes. But I love to break away from the more traditional flavor pairings, as I have with this sweet-and-sour combination. It's like looking far away, to Asia, for inspiration. At the same time, the salad showcases one of my home region's most popular cheeses: Afuega'l Pitu from Asturias. Creamy, with a natural, earthy aroma, it is considered one of the finest cheeses made in Spain.

Ensalada de espárragos blancos

Soft and crunchy white asparagus salad

SERVES 4

4 TABLESPOONS SPANISH EXTRA-VIRGIN OLIVE OIL

1 TABLESPOON SHERRY VINEGAR

SALT TO TASTE

2 16-OUNCE CANS SPANISH WHITE ASPARAGUS, DRAINED

6–8 FRESH WHITE ASPARAGUS SPEARS, TRIMMED AND PEELED

1 ORANGE

2 OUNCES RONCAL (SPANISH SHEEP'S-MILK CHEESE FROM NAVARRE)

FRESH EDIBLE FLOWERS (OPTIONAL)

1 TEASPOON CHOPPED CHERVIL, FOR GARNISH

Whisk together the olive oil and vinegar in a mixing bowl. Season to taste with salt and set aside. Cut the canned asparagus spears in thirds and divide the pieces among 4 plates.

Slice fresh asparagus thinly on an angle and set aside.

Slice off the top and bottom of the orange. Using a sharp knife, cut down the sides of the orange to remove all of the peel and pith. Slice along the sides of each membrane and pull out the segments. Arrange the segments around the canned asparagus spears on each plate. Divide the asparagus slices among the plates. Drizzle some dressing over the salads. Use a vegetable peeler to slice ribbons of cheese onto each salad. Drizzle with a little more dressing, garnish with edible flowers and fresh chervil, if you like, and serve.

There's nothing quite so special as eating fresh asparagus in Navarre, just as the beautiful spears break through the dirt and before they feel the warmth of the approaching summer. Even when they are still dirty from the earth, their flavor is one of the freshest I've ever tasted. In this dish, we are trying to re-create that first bite into the crunchy asparagus, at the same time as pairing it with canned white asparagus, which is one of Navarre's best-known vegetable products. Think crunchiness, sweetness, and softness.

José's Tip:

Roncal is a slightly nutty and firm sheep's-milk cheese. If you can't find it, try Manchego, the classic Spanish cheese. If fresh white asparagus is out of season, you can use fresh green asparagus instead.

"Esqueixada" de bacalao

Shredded salt cod with tomatoes and olives

SERVES 4

8 OUNCES SALT COD (SEE TIP)

4 RIPE PLUM TOMATOES

1 TABLESPOON SPANISH EXTRA-VIRGIN OLIVE OIL, PLUS MORE FOR DRIZZLING

¼ CUP PITTED BLACK OLIVES

2 TEASPOONS THINLY SLICED SCALLION

SALT TO TASTE

2 TEASPOONS MINCED CHIVES

Put the cod in a large bowl, skin side up. Cover with water and refrigerate for 36 hours, changing the water at least 3 times to remove the salt. Drain the cod and pat dry with a paper towel. With your fingers, shred the cod into small strips and set aside.

Slice the tomatoes in half. Place a grater over a mixing bowl. Rub the cut surface of the tomatoes over the grater until all of the flesh is grated. Discard the skins. Strain the tomato pulp through a fine-mesh strainer, then stir in 1 tablespoon of the olive oil and set aside.

Spread a thin layer of shredded salt cod across 4 plates. Spoon a layer of the tomato pulp on top of the cod. Arrange the olives around each plate and sprinkle with sliced scallion. Drizzle each plate with olive oil, season with salt, and garnish with the chives.

José's Tip:
It is important to use the highest-quality salt cod you can find for this dish. If you buy it already desalted, you can skip the first step of soaking the fish. To test your cod's readiness, pinch off a bit of fish from the center of the piece and taste. You'll find the time needed to release the salt will vary depending on the thickness of the fish.

In many markets in Catalonia, you'll find stands selling salt cod, or what we call *bacalao*. The cod is often sold from small water baths, with the bacalao at different stages of desalination. Lucky for us, in Spain and the United States, there's a company called Giraldo that sells the best salt cod at the perfect moment of desalination, ready to be served.

Ensalada de lentejas con queso Valdeón

Lentil salad with blue Valdeón cheese

SERVES 4

FOR THE SALAD

1 CUP DRIED FRENCH GREEN LENTILS

½ ONION

½ HEAD OF GARLIC, PAPERY OUTER SKIN REMOVED

1 BAY LEAF

2 TABLESPOONS SPANISH EXTRA-VIRGIN OLIVE OIL

1 TEASPOON SALT

½ CUP DICED GREEN BELL PEPPER

½ CUP DICED RED BELL PEPPER

½ CUP DICED, SEEDED PLUM TOMATOES

1 SHALLOT, DICED

FOR THE DRESSING

3 TABLESPOONS SPANISH EXTRA-VIRGIN OLIVE OIL

2 TABLESPOONS SHERRY VINEGAR

2 TEASPOONS SEA SALT

2 TABLESPOONS CHOPPED CHIVES

2 OUNCES VALDEÓN (SPANISH BLUE CHEESE FROM CASTILLA Y LEÓN), CRUMBLED

Prepare the salad: Put the lentils, onion, garlic, bay leaf, olive oil, salt, and 4 cups water in a medium-deep pot and bring to a boil over medium-high heat. Reduce the heat to a simmer and cook the lentils until tender, about 20 minutes. Strain the lentils, reserving the cooking liquid. Pour a little of the liquid over the lentils to prevent them from drying out. Discard the onion, garlic, and bay leaf.

Return the remaining cooking liquid to the pot and bring to a boil over medium-high heat. Boil until it has reduced to ½ cup, about 20 minutes. Set the reduced liquid aside to cool.

Put the lentils, peppers, tomatoes, and shallot into a mixing bowl.

Prepare the dressing: Whisk the olive oil, vinegar, salt, and reduced lentil cooking liquid together in a separate mixing bowl.

Pour the dressing over the salad, sprinkle with chives, and mix well. Divide the salad among 4 bowls and garnish with the cheese.

José's Tip:
A Stilton or other good-quality blue cheese may be substituted for the Valdeón.

Lentils remind me of the stew we ate at home at the end of the month, when money was running short. Although it was a meal that cost very little, I always looked forward to the delicious and hearty stew, with a little bit of carrot, garlic, and onion. Best of all, any leftovers made a perfect salad the next day. The acidity of the vinegar elevates this humble dish to the point where it's difficult to stop after one bite; you'll find you always want more.

Cojondongo

Extremaduran cold tomato bread salad

SERVES 4

- 2 THICK SLICES RUSTIC BREAD (ABOUT 4 OUNCES)
- 6 TABLESPOONS SPANISH EXTRA-VIRGIN OLIVE OIL
- 6 RIPE PLUM TOMATOES
- ½ GARLIC CLOVE, PEELED
- ¼ TEASPOON SWEET PIMENTÓN (SPANISH SMOKED PAPRIKA)
- 1 TABLESPOON CHOPPED FRESH FLAT-LEAF PARSLEY
- SEA SALT TO TASTE
- 1 TABLESPOON SHERRY VINEGAR
- 1 GREEN BELL PEPPER, SEEDED AND DICED
- 1 SCALLION, THINLY SLICED
- 1 CUP QUARTERED GREEN OLIVES

As far as I'm concerned, Spain is the king of cold dishes—and this example is a prime reason. To some people, cojondongo would be considered a thick soup, but it is really a refreshing summer salad. Apart from its freshness, what I like most about the dish is its name, which has no literal translation.

Preheat the oven to 400°F.

Cut the bread into 1-inch cubes and toss in a mixing bowl with 2 tablespoons of the olive oil. Spread the bread on a sheet pan and bake on the middle rack until golden brown, about 5 minutes. Set the croutons aside to cool.

Cut 4 of the tomatoes in half. Place a grater over a mixing bowl. Rub the cut surface of the tomatoes over the grater until all of the flesh is grated; discard the skin. Spoon the tomato pulp into a fine-mesh strainer set over a large bowl. Allow the pulp to drain for 30 minutes. Reserve the drained pulp. Dice the remaining tomatoes.

Using a mortar and pestle, smash the garlic together with the pimentón, parsley, and a pinch of salt to make a smooth paste. (The salt stops the garlic from slipping at the bottom of the mortar as you pound it down.) Whisk 3 tablespoons of the olive oil and the vinegar together in a small bowl, and then stir in the garlic-parsley paste.

In a mixing bowl, combine the croutons, peppers, diced tomatoes, scallion, and olives and toss together. Pour in the dressing and mix well. To serve, spread the reserved tomato pulp on a serving platter and drizzle with the remaining tablespoon of olive oil. Top with the bread salad and season to taste with salt.

Pipirrana con mojama

Pepper, onion, cucumber, and tomato salad with cured tuna loin

SERVES 4

3 TABLESPOONS SPANISH EXTRA-VIRGIN OLIVE OIL

1 TABLESPOON SHERRY VINEGAR

SEA SALT TO TASTE

½ CUCUMBER

1 GREEN BELL PEPPER, SEEDED AND MINCED

1 RIPE PLUM TOMATO, SEEDED AND MINCED

8 CHERRY TOMATOES, HALVED

1 OUNCE THINLY SLICED MOJAMA (SPANISH SALT-CURED TUNA LOIN), ABOUT 12 SLICES

1 SCALLION, THINLY SLICED

FRESH CHERVIL SPRIGS

In a bowl, whisk together the olive oil and vinegar. Season to taste with salt and set the dressing aside.

Peel the cucumber and, using an apple corer, remove the seeds in one piece. Cut the seed core into 1-inch pieces and set aside. Finely dice the remaining cucumber. Put the diced cucumber, the pepper, and the plum tomato in a mixing bowl. Toss with 1 tablespoon of the dressing and season to taste with salt.

To serve, spread spoonfuls of the minced vegetables over 4 plates. Place 4 cherry tomato halves and 4 cucumber cores on top of each serving. Lay the mojama slices across the tomatoes, sprinkle with scallions and chervil, and drizzle with a little more of the dressing.

The almadraba system of netting is an ancient fishing tradition still practiced in Spain. Each May, it yields a great catch of tuna, netted where the Atlantic meets the Mediterranean off the coast of Barbate and Zahara de los Atúnes in the province of Cadíz. For centuries, the fishermen have air-dried the best cuts of tuna to create the dark and intense mojama. This recipe is dedicated to those fishermen who bring us the fresh seafood we can't live without. Please don't leave any fish on your plate; people have risked their lives to bring it to you.

José's Tip:
Mojama is available online and at some specialty food shops. Be sure to slice it very thin when serving. If you can't find mojama, good-quality anchovy fillets are a great and flavorful substitute.

Ensalada de alcachofa cruda

Raw artichoke salad

SERVES 4

8 MEDIUM ARTICHOKES

1 BUNCH FRESH FLAT-LEAF PARSLEY

2 ORANGES

4 TABLESPOONS SPANISH EXTRA-VIRGIN OLIVE OIL

1 TABLESPOON SHERRY VINEGAR

4 CUPS FRISÉE

SEA SALT TO TASTE

Artichokes seem exotic to some people, but they are hard to resist after the first bite. There are many ways to cook them, but the best way to enjoy them—especially when they are small and tender—is to eat them raw. (The second-best way is to play "Loves me, loves me not" with all the leaves. Just make sure you end with "Loves me.")

Use a serrated knife to cut off the top half of each artichoke. Break off and discard all of the exterior leaves until you reach the pale green, tender center leaves. Pry apart the leaves with your fingers and use a spoon to scrape out the white, hairy center (choke). Use a small knife to peel away the tough outer layer around the base of the artichoke and stem, until you reach the soft white flesh. Don't be afraid to remove most of the artichoke. Put the trimmed artichoke into a large bowl of cold water. Add the parsley to stop the artichoke from oxidizing and coloring.

Using a mandoline, thinly slice 4 of the artichoke bottoms and discard the stems. Return the artichoke slices to the cold parsley water.

Bring a medium pot of salted water to a boil and add the 4 whole trimmed artichokes. Cook until tender, about 8 minutes. Drain and, once cooled, quarter them and add to the cold parsley water.

Using the small holes of a grater or a microplane, zest half of one of the oranges. Then slice off the top and bottom of each orange and cut down the sides to remove all of the peel and pith. Holding the oranges over a mixing bowl to catch any juices, slice along the sides of each membrane and pull out the segments.

José's Tip:
Don't be tempted to put lemon in the water with your artichokes. Parsley is all you need to keep the artichokes from oxidizing and turning brown. Lemon juice will give the artichokes a bitter flavor.

Whisk the olive oil, vinegar, and 1 teaspoon of the reserved orange juice together in a bowl. Drain the artichokes and gently pat dry with paper towel. Put the thinly sliced artichokes into a large mixing bowl and toss with 1 tablespoon of the dressing, then arrange the slices on 4 plates. Put the quartered artichoke bottoms into the same mixing bowl and toss with another tablespoon of the dressing. Arrange the quartered artichokes over the slices. Add the frisée and orange segments to the same mixing bowl and toss with another tablespoon of the dressing. Arrange the greens on top of the artichokes, drizzle with a little more of the dressing, and season to taste with salt.

Ensalada murciana con queso Murcia al vino

Drunken goat cheese and tomato salad

SERVES 4

4 RIPE BEEFSTEAK TOMATOES

4 TABLESPOONS SPANISH EXTRA-VIRGIN OLIVE OIL

SEA SALT TO TASTE

4 RIPE PLUM TOMATOES

1 TABLESPOON PEDRO XIMÉNEZ (PX) VINEGAR, OR SPANISH AGED SHERRY VINEGAR

8 OUNCES MURCIA AL VINO (RED WINE-SOAKED SPANISH GOAT CHEESE), CUT INTO ½-INCH STICKS

½ CUP EMPELTRE OLIVES OR OTHER GOOD-QUALITY BLACK OLIVES, PITTED

FRESH THYME SPRIGS

FRESH CHERVIL SPRIGS

Using an apple corer, cut out the centers of the beefsteak tomatoes. Trim off the stem end of the cores, cut the cores in half, and set aside. Slice the tomatoes in half. Place a grater over a large mixing bowl. Rub the cut surface of the tomatoes over the grater until all the flesh is grated. Discard the skin. Season the tomato pulp with 1 tablespoon of the olive oil and a little salt and set aside.

Using a sharp knife, slice off the top and bottom of each plum tomato. Locate the fleshy dividing wall of one segment inside the tomato. Slice alongside the dividing wall and open up the flesh of the tomato to expose the seeds. Remove the seeds and their pulp by slicing around the core of the tomato. Set the seeds aside. Your aim is to keep the pulp of the seeds together to create tomato-seed "fillets" that are separate from the firmer tomato flesh. Finely dice the tomato flesh and set aside.

Whisk the remaining 3 tablespoons olive oil and the vinegar together in a bowl and season to taste with salt. Spread the grated tomato pulp on a serving platter. Sprinkle the diced plum tomatoes on top of the pulp. Arrange the reserved beefsteak tomato cores on top. Place the tomato-seed "fillets" around the platter. Top with the cheese and the olives and drizzle with the dressing. Garnish with thyme, chervil, and sea salt.

Using wine both to flavor and to conserve goat cheese is an unusual method that creates a delicious, light, and creamy cheese. The cheeses from the Jumilla region in Murcia are becoming more widely available in stores across America. My children love it; see if yours will too.

José's Tip:

Tomato seeds are so different from the tomato flesh in texture, taste, and look. To me, they are a hidden caviar. Yes, it's more work to separate them. But along the way, you're exploring the wonders of the tomato and transforming your salad into something truly special.

In Spain, we have soups for all climates and all classes. The cold soups of southern Spain, from tomato gazpacho to the almond and garlic ajo blanco, are renowned around the world. Why cold soups? One obvious reason is the heat of the region: Cold soups cool you down while they replenish your body with salty water. In Roman times, Spaniards drank a lot of what they called almond milk, made by crushing nuts with garlic and salt and mixing them with water. That is the ancestor of the humble ajo blanco. But in the center and north of Spain, soups are big, hot meals, like the cocido of Madrid. This stew mixes ingredients from every part of Spain: vegetables, legumes, meats. When the stew is ready, after many hours of cooking, the people of Madrid eat it in separate courses: first the broth, followed by the vegetables, and finally the meats. If cocido is the soup of the people, then the consommé at Madrid's first formal restaurant, Lhardy, is the soup of the upper classes. It's a refined, clear broth, served with a splash of favorite sherry, just as it was when the restaurant opened its doors more than a century ago.

soups

28,40
AZA DE
ABEL II
BERNA
1996
COLATERIA
SAN GINES
5
AÑO 1929
A DE TO

madrid

Madrid is a fascinating and vibrant city and region. If you have a chance to visit, make sure you take the time to drive out of the city, in any direction, to see the beautiful countryside; you'll find wonderful history to explore and restaurants to enjoy. In Aranjuez, just south of the capital, you can tour the magnificent palace that was once the spring escape for Spain's kings and queens. The town inspired Joaquín Rodrigo's guitar masterpiece, the *Concierto de Aranjuez*, but I find its great produce just as inspiring—especially the wonderfully sweet strawberries that were first planted there five hundred years ago.

I didn't always see Madrid through the eyes of a chef. Soccer fans (and that describes most Spaniards) know that Madrid is home to one of the greatest teams in the world: Real Madrid. As a native of Barcelona, who grew up as a devoted fan of that city's team, I feel an intense rivalry. On top of that, there are historical reasons for tensions between Spain's capital city and Barcelona, the capital of Catalonia. Of course, it's a friendly rivalry—the kind of passion that makes Spain so vibrant.

Those feelings changed after I spent four months in Madrid when I was nineteen, working in what was probably one of the hottest restaurants in Spain at the time: El Cenador del Prado, owned by the talented chef Tomás Herranz. Herranz (who sadly has passed away) had cooked for some time in the States and, as a young cook, I was impressed with the forward-thinking ideas he had developed, especially during his time at Café San Martín in New York. This was an exciting time to be working with Herranz. Madrid was going through a special intellectual and cultural phase, which was called *La Movida*. Historically, Madrid has always been home to avant-garde thinkers and intellectuals, and this latest movement was inspired by the revolutionary ideas of young artists like the movie director Pedro Almodóvar. My days were spent working in the restaurant. My nights were spent partying at bars.

For me, Madrid has always been a mixture of high and low culture—of museums of art and temples to food, a city of the very best restaurants and wonderful street food, like the squid sandwiches of the Plaza Mayor. Sixteen or seventeen years ago, ethnic restaurants, where you could eat food like falafel and kebabs, were just opening in Madrid. As much as I loved these new flavors, I also loved the places that had been open for centuries, like Lhardy, which always seemed to me like one of the city's great palaces, like the Palacio Real. Today, Madrid is also home to my TV show in Spain, *Vamos a Cocinar*, which was my successful attempt to reintroduce Spanish home cooks to the great food of their own country. To many tourists, Madrid may look like a historical artifact, but it's still a creative center for Spaniards who are looking to the future.

Gazpacho al estilo de Patricia

Patricia's Gazpacho

SERVES 4 TO 6

FOR THE SOUP

1 CUCUMBER, PEELED AND CHOPPED

1 GREEN BELL PEPPER, SEEDED AND CHOPPED

3 POUNDS RIPE PLUM TOMATOES, CHOPPED

2 GARLIC CLOVES

¼ CUP SHERRY VINEGAR

¼ CUP OLOROSO SHERRY

¾ CUP SPANISH EXTRA-VIRGIN OLIVE OIL

FOR THE GARNISH

2 1-INCH-THICK SLICES OF RUSTIC BREAD

¼ CUP SPANISH EXTRA-VIRGIN OLIVE OIL

½ CUCUMBER

12 CHERRY TOMATOES, HALVED

SEA SALT TO TASTE

Prepare the soup: Combine the cucumber, pepper, tomatoes, garlic, vinegar, sherry, olive oil, and 2 cups water in a food processor or blender. (You may need to do this in batches, depending on the capacity of your blender.) Purée the ingredients until everything is well blended into a thick pink liquid. Pour the gazpacho through a medium-hole strainer into a pitcher. Refrigerate for about 30 minutes.

Prepare the garnish: Preheat the oven to 400°F. Cut the bread into 1-inch cubes and toss in a mixing bowl with 2 tablespoons of the olive oil. Spread the bread cubes on a baking sheet and bake on the middle rack until golden brown, about 5 minutes. Set the croutons aside to cool.

When you are ready to serve, slice the cucumber into ribbons with a vegetable peeler. Put a few croutons, cherry tomato halves, and cucumber ribbons in each bowl and pour the gazpacho over them. Drizzle with the remaining 2 tablespoons of olive oil and sprinkle with salt.

I think this gazpacho recipe, created by my wife, Patricia, must have been made in thousands of homes across America by now. It was published in the *Washington Post*, the *Wall Street Journal*, and *Food & Wine*, and I've also made it with my friends on the *Today* show on NBC. If you missed it somehow, you'll be glad to have it now; it's the perfect gazpacho. (And just in case you're wondering, my wife is *not* looking for a job in a restaurant.)

Sopa fría de queso Idiazábal y setas silvestres

Cold soup of Idiazábal cheese with wild mushrooms

SERVES 4

FOR THE SOUP

1 TABLESPOON SPANISH EXTRA-VIRGIN OLIVE OIL

½ CUP DICED SPANISH ONIONS

1 GARLIC CLOVE, PEELED AND MINCED

2 TABLESPOONS DRY WHITE WINE, PREFERABLY SPANISH TXAKOLÍ

¾ CUP HEAVY CREAM

3 OUNCES IDIAZÁBAL (SMOKY-FLAVORED BASQUE SHEEP'S-MILK CHEESE), GRATED

¾ CUP FLAT MINERAL OR FILTERED WATER

FOR THE GARNISH

2 TABLESPOONS SPANISH EXTRA-VIRGIN OLIVE OIL

2 OUNCES WILD MUSHROOMS, SUCH AS CHANTERELLES OR OYSTER, LARGER MUSHROOMS HALVED

1 OUNCE IDIAZÁBAL CHEESE

4 WALNUT HALVES

LEAVES OF 2 FRESH THYME SPRIGS

Prepare the soup: In a deep pot, heat the olive oil over medium heat. Add the onions and cook until they are translucent, about 10 minutes, stirring occasionally. Add the garlic to the onions and cook for 4 more minutes, then add the wine and cook for 2 minutes, or until the alcohol is mostly evaporated.

Add the cream, cheese, and mineral water to the pot. Bring the soup to a simmer over low heat and stir for 1 minute. Be careful not to let the cheese stick to the bottom of the pot. Remove the pot from the heat, cover, and set aside to cool for 15 minutes.

Pour the soup through a fine mesh strainer into a large bowl. Cover and refrigerate until the soup is well chilled, about 3 hours.

Prepare the garnish: Heat 1 tablespoon of the olive oil in a small sauté pan over medium-high heat. Add the mushrooms and cook for 2 minutes, then set aside to cool.

Shave the cheese with a vegetable peeler into 4 soup bowls. Divide the mushrooms and walnut halves among the bowls. Drizzle the bowls with the remaining tablespoon olive oil, then ladle the cold soup into the bowls. Sprinkle with thyme leaves.

I love dishes that showcase familiar ingredients in unexpected ways. Cheese is often added for taste in hot food, as it is in omelets. Making a soup with cheese is a great way to add a deep flavor. Serving cheese soup cold adds an unusual twist.

José's Tip:
If you can't find Idiazábal cheese, try another sheep's-milk cheese, such as Manchego.

Ajo blanco con higos y almendras

Cold almond and garlic soup with figs and Marcona almonds

SERVES 4 TO 6

1½ POUNDS BLANCHED ALMONDS

6 CUPS FLAT MINERAL OR FILTERED WATER

2 GARLIC CLOVES

¾ CUP AGED SHERRY VINEGAR, PLUS 1 TABLESPOON

2½ CUPS SPANISH EXTRA-VIRGIN OLIVE OIL, PLUS 2 TABLESPOONS

3 SLICES OF RUSTIC BREAD, CRUSTS REMOVED, ABOUT 2 OUNCES

4 FRESH BLACK FIGS, QUARTERED

4 TABLESPOONS ROUGHLY CHOPPED SPANISH MARCONA ALMONDS

1 TABLESPOON CHOPPED CHIVES

Put the blanched almonds into a bowl, cover with the mineral water, and let soak overnight.

Bring 2 cups of water to a boil in a small pot over high heat. Add the garlic and boil for 1 minute, then drain the garlic and cool.

Drain the soaked almonds, reserving the soaking liquid, and put them in a blender or food processor. Add the garlic, reserved soaking liquid, ¾ cup of the sherry vinegar, 2½ cups of the olive oil, and bread, and purée until smooth. Place a colander over a large bowl and line it with cheesecloth. Pour the soup into the colander. Once most of the liquid has passed through the colander, gather the cheesecloth around the remaining solids and squeeze gently to release as much of the liquid as possible. Discard the solids. Pour the soup into a pitcher and chill for 30 minutes.

To serve, divide the fig pieces and Marcona almonds among soup bowls. Pour in the cold soup, sprinkle with chopped chives, and drizzle with the remaining 1 tablespoon vinegar and 2 tablespoons olive oil.

José's Tip:
Soaking the almonds overnight is important. This step helps bring out the natural milk of the almonds.

Figs and almonds are two very Mediterranean ingredients. Together they make this simple but interesting cold soup—a glimpse of what people ate in the south of Spain before the introduction of new ingredients from the Americas. Here we combine regular almonds with the great Marcona variety, which are rounder, smoother, sweeter, and more expensive than the everyday nut. We save the Marcona for their flavor at the end; the regular almonds are blended into the body of the soup.

Consomé a la Lhardy

Lhardy's famous consommé

SERVES 4 TO 8

- 1 TABLESPOON SPANISH EXTRA-VIRGIN OLIVE OIL
- 1 LARGE SPANISH ONION, CUT INTO ½-INCH RINGS
- 2 POUNDS VEAL BONES
- 1 3-POUND CHICKEN, CUT INTO PIECES
- 1 8-OUNCE FRESH (NOT SMOKED) HAM HOCK
- ½ POUND CARROTS
- 2 CELERY STALKS
- 1 LARGE LEEK, HALVED AND WELL RINSED
- ½ POUND RIPE PLUM TOMATOES
- ¼ CUP COARSE SEA SALT
- 10 EGG WHITES

Heat the olive oil in a large sauté pan over medium-high heat. Add the onion slices and sear on both sides, about 10 minutes (see Tip below).

Transfer the onion to a large stockpot. Add the veal bones, chicken pieces, ham hock, carrots, celery, leek, tomatoes, and salt and cover with 2 gallons water. Bring to a boil over a medium-high flame, then reduce the heat to low and simmer for at least 3 hours, occasionally skimming off any foam that forms on top. For a stronger broth, cook up to 5 hours. Strain the broth; set the chicken and ham hock aside and reserve for another use. Discard the remaining solids. Rinse the stockpot and return the strained broth to the pot.

In a large mixing bowl, whisk the egg whites until they are foamy. Add the egg whites to the broth. Stirring constantly to prevent the egg whites from sticking to the bottom of the pot, slowly bring the broth back to a boil over medium-high heat. Once the broth reaches a boil, reduce the heat to low and simmer for 1 more hour. The egg whites will rise to the top and form a raft, picking up any debris left in the broth. Do not stir the broth once the raft forms, or the stock will become cloudy. Spoon out the raft carefully with a slotted spoon and discard. Strain the broth through a cheesecloth-lined colander into a soup tureen.

José's Tip:

To give your consommé a deep rich color, let the onion slices brown. To make this recipe correctly, you need to make a lot. You can serve half of the soup and freeze the rest. The consommé can keep in the freezer, sealed in an airtight container, for up to 3 months. The reserved boiled chicken can be used for the empanada recipe (page 192).

When I was studying the history of gastronomy in school, I learned that the restaurant Lhardy was an important meeting place for philosophers, politicians, and scientists in the nineteenth century. Now when I open the door and walk into this magnificent place, I have an emotional reaction. For me, nothing surpasses the simplicity of their consommé, served with a splash of one of the great Spanish sherries that sits on the shelves behind the counter. I remember the day I shot part of my TV show there, and I drank about twelve cups of consommé. Every one of them had a drop of sherry. Just as well it was the last shoot of the day.

Porrusalda

Basque-style leek and potato soup

SERVES 4 TO 6

½ CUP SPANISH EXTRA-VIRGIN OLIVE OIL

2 GARLIC CLOVES

3 LARGE LEEKS (WHITE PARTS ONLY), CUT INTO ½-INCH RINGS AND RINSED WELL

2 LARGE RUSSET POTATOES, PEELED AND CUT INTO 1-INCH CUBES

SEA SALT TO TASTE

1 8-OUNCE COD FILLET, CUT INTO 4 PIECES

2 OUNCES JAMÓN SERRANO (SPANISH CURED HAM), THINLY SLICED

1 SCALLION (GREEN PART ONLY), THINLY SLICED

Heat 2 tablespoons of the olive oil in a 12-quart stockpot over medium heat. Add the garlic and brown lightly on all sides, about 2 minutes. Add the leeks and potatoes and cook until lightly golden, about 5 minutes, then add 2 quarts water. Cover the pot, reduce the heat to low, and simmer for 45 minutes.

Working in batches, transfer the soup to a blender or food processor and blend until smooth, drizzling in ¼ cup of the olive oil. Season to taste with salt.

Pour the soup through a medium-hole strainer back into the pot. Bring the soup to a simmer over medium-low heat, add the cod fillets, and cook for 6 to 8 minutes. Divide the soup and the cod pieces among shallow bowls and garnish with a piece of jamón Serrano, some scallion, and drizzle with the remaining 2 tablespoons of olive oil.

I admit it: I'm more than a little patriotic when it comes to food. One of the first soups I learned to make was vichyssoise, a cold leek and potato soup from France. So I was very happy to learn a few months later about this classic Spanish soup of leeks and cod, which is popular in the Basque country.

Salmorejo

Cold tomato soup with ham and hard-boiled egg

SERVES 4

FOR THE SOUP

- 1 POUND RIPE PLUM TOMATOES, QUARTERED
- 1 GARLIC CLOVE, PEELED
- 2 TABLESPOONS SHERRY VINEGAR
- ¼ CUP SPANISH EXTRA-VIRGIN OLIVE OIL, PLUS 2 TABLESPOONS
- 2 SLICES STALE RUSTIC BREAD, CRUSTS REMOVED, CUT INTO CHUNKS, ABOUT 1 OUNCE
- SEA SALT TO TASTE

FOR THE GARNISH

- 2 TABLESPOONS SPANISH EXTRA-VIRGIN OLIVE OIL
- 1 TABLESPOON SHERRY VINEGAR
- 2 HARD-BOILED EGGS, PEELED AND HALVED
- 4 THIN SLICES JAMÓN SERRANO (SPANISH CURED HAM)

Prepare the soup: Combine the tomatoes, garlic, vinegar, ¼ cup of the olive oil, and bread in a blender. Purée until the mixture is smooth and has the consistency of a thick soup. Continue puréeing and slowly add the remaining 2 tablespoons of olive oil. Pour into a large bowl, season to taste with salt, and refrigerate for 15 minutes.

To serve, ladle the chilled soup into bowls. Drizzle each bowl with olive oil and a little sherry vinegar. Place the eggs and jamón on a serving platter. Use the garnishes to dip into the soup.

This soup is an homage to the times when every bit of food was used in the kitchen and nothing was thrown away. I love the way the old bread softens with the other ingredients. I also love the history of this dish: It's a perfect combination of an Old World recipe of bread, garlic, and vinegar, lifted by the New World addition of tomatoes. The result is a thick soup you eat as a dip with the garnishes.

"Snacks" may sound like a stopgap between meals, but in Spain they are an everyday part of dining and a way of life. Nowadays, many people around the world know Spanish food through tapas, the small snack-like dishes that are so popular in Barcelona and Seville—and also in Washington, D.C., at my three restaurants called Jaleo. But in the northern region of the Basque country, snacks take a different form called pintxos—typically, small rounds of bread with fantastic toppings, all skewered together with a cocktail stick. For Basque people, bar-hopping means sharing a few pintxos with friends at one bar, then walking down the street to continue the meal at the next bar. Drinking is just part of the experience; the real attention is focused on savoring the food. To prove the point, the bars themselves are covered with plates of pintxos (in contrast to the tapas bars of the south, where you pick from a long menu). Given the complex creations you find in many pintxo bars, the word *snack* hardly does them justice. They now represent a miniature cuisine, influenced by the new wave of Basque chefs, and their creators are rightly acknowledged with national culinary prizes.

snacks

país vasco

My mother was born in Barakaldo, a northern Basque town, and for many years that was my only connection to the Basque country—although to many Spaniards, my face suggests that I have Basque roots. Then, when I was seventeen, my friend Albert Adrià recommended a Basque restaurant in Barcelona called Chicoa. It was there that my love for Basque cooking and the Basque country (or, as we call it, País Vasco) was born.

There's so much to love when it comes to the food of the Basque region, a mysterious and distinctive part of northern Spain. There are wonderful cheeses like Idiazábal, great wines like Txakolí, and the eye-popping snacks called pintxos. There are exceptional fish dishes, like Marmitako, which uses the northern tuna, or Bacalao al Pil Pil, which uses the legendary Basque salt cod. There's humble food like the railway workers' stew called putxera, and the high-end cuisine of my heroes at some of the best restaurants in the world, especially the group of chefs led by Juan Mari Arzak, who spearheaded a renaissance of traditional Basque cooking.

Juan Mari has become one of the most famous chefs in the world, and just the mention of his name is enough to make a lesser cook like me sit up straight. In 1992, I was living in Manhattan and learning about Arzak from a young Basque chef whom I knew only as Oscar. He told me fascinating stories about his time working with Arzak—tales so amazing that I thought I was listening to a Basque version of *Alice in Wonderland.* I didn't know whether they were true or not, and didn't want to; sometimes you just want to believe.

Late one night, after having maybe one too many drinks, I picked up the phone and called Arzak's restaurant. (Remember, he was *the* chef in Spain at the time.) I asked for Juan Mari and said it was José Andrés from New York calling. I guess the words *New York* open many doors, because Juan Mari himself picked up the phone. I was nervous, but I quickly found the courage to introduce myself, arrogantly informing him that I was a chef and was interested in working for him on a temporary basis.

Graciously but firmly, he explained a long list of chefs was waiting for the chance to *stage* with him. Because my motto in life is that failure is only the road to success, I never saw his nicely delivered "no" as a failure. We actually ended the conversation on a pleasant note, and I was excited to have spoken with the great Arzak. It would be naïve to tell you I'm a better cook today because of the conversation, but I do believe people can pass their aura to others and that certain connections can influence you positively. A few years later, when I was a well-established chef in America, I met Juan Mari in San Sebastián, and he still remembered the strange call from the brazen young chef in New York. Since then, I've shared many good times with him and his daughter Elena, and when he comes to America, Juan Mari often asks me to act as his translator, as I did at one extraordinary dinner with Paul Bocuse and Alain Ducasse. Since that first phone call, my admiration for the man has only grown, as has my appreciation for the Basque country and its culinary heritage.

Basque country cooking is known for its fresh vegetables and seafood, not least because of the region's wonderful farms and its historic fishing fleet. As a result, Basque people are famous for their high standards in food, and Basque cooking features complex and unusual combinations of ingredients and flavors. There are many great chefs in the Basque region, like Pedro Subijana, Martín Berasategui, and Andoni Luis Aduriz. But I believe Arzak—with his humble devotion to tradition and his constant pursuit of creativity—represents the spirit of the Basque country better than anyone else.

Pimientos del piquillo rellenos de queso Roncal

Seared piquillo peppers stuffed with Roncal cheese

SERVES 4

5 TABLESPOONS SPANISH EXTRA-VIRGIN OLIVE OIL

1 TABLESPOON PEDRO XIMÉNEZ (PX) VINEGAR, OR SPANISH AGED SHERRY VINEGAR

1 TABLESPOON MINCED SHALLOT

½ SCALLION (WHITE PART ONLY), THINLY SLICED

SEA SALT AND FRESHLY CRACKED BLACK PEPPER

8 PIQUILLO PEPPERS

4 OUNCES RONCAL (SPANISH SHEEP'S-MILK CHEESE), CUT INTO 2-INCH STICKS

FRESH THYME SPRIGS

FRESH PARSLEY SPRIGS

Whisk 4 tablespoons of the olive oil together with the vinegar, shallot, and scallion in a mixing bowl. Season with salt and pepper. Cut a small slit into each piquillo pepper and slide a stick of cheese into each.

Heat the remaining tablespoon of olive oil in a medium sauté pan over high heat. Add the peppers and brown on both sides until the cheese begins to melt, about 30 seconds. Transfer the peppers to a serving platter, drizzle with dressing, and sprinkle with leaves from the thyme and parsley sprigs. Serve immediately.

Recently, it seems as though chefs are stuffing sweet piquillo peppers from Lodosa with every single thing you can imagine. Although many of the stuffings are tasty, they're also so complicated that they require a long cooking process. Here, the piquillo pepper is simply matched with a great cheese, used just as is. This is a tapa that home cooks can create without breaking a sweat.

José's Tip:
You could just as easily stuff a piquillo with another of your favorite Spanish cheeses to create your own tapa in no time.

Aceitunas aliñadas con hierbas

Herb-marinated olives

SERVES 4 TO 6

1 ORANGE

5 GARLIC CLOVES

1 CUP EMPELTRE OR OTHER CURED BLACK OLIVES

1 CUP ARBEQUINA OR OTHER SMALL CURED GREEN OLIVES

1 CUP MANZANILLA OLIVES (LARGE GREEN OLIVES ALSO KNOWN AS SPANISH OLIVES)

2 BAY LEAVES

3 FRESH THYME SPRIGS, BROKEN UP WITH YOUR FINGERS

2 FRESH ROSEMARY SPRIGS, BROKEN UP WITH YOUR FINGERS

1 CUP SPANISH EXTRA-VIRGIN OLIVE OIL, PREFERABLY AN ARBEQUINA VARIETY

2 TABLESPOONS MARCONA ALMONDS

COARSE SEA SALT TO TASTE

Using a vegetable peeler, remove the zest from the orange, then squeeze the juice into a bowl. Split the garlic cloves by placing them on a chopping board and pressing down hard with the heel of your hand or the flat side of a kitchen knife. Put the garlic, olives, bay leaves, thyme, and rosemary into a large mixing bowl and add the olive oil, orange juice, and zest. Mix well. (You can also combine the garlic, olives, herbs, orange juice, zest, and olive oil in a plastic container with a lid and simply shake.)

Cover the bowl with plastic wrap and marinate at room temperature for at least 4 hours or refrigerate overnight. The olives can be kept in the refrigerator for up to 1 week. Be sure to allow the olives to come to room temperature before serving. When you're ready to serve, garnish with the almonds and sea salt.

Olives grow throughout Spain, and the varieties from each region have distinct flavors. Pick your favorite olives for this dish—as long as they're from Spain. Here I've used a selection of the country's best varieties.

Tostada de Garrotxa

Tomato toast with Garrotxa cheese

SERVES 4

4 SLICES RUSTIC BREAD

2 RIPE PLUM TOMATOES, HALVED

2 TABLESPOONS SPANISH EXTRA-VIRGIN OLIVE OIL

4 OUNCES GARROTXA (SPANISH GOAT'S-MILK CHEESE FROM CATALONIA), THINLY SLICED

SEA SALT TO TASTE

Toast the bread in a broiler or over a grill. When the bread is browned, rub each piece of toast with the cut surface of a tomato half until all the flesh is grated. Discard the skins. Arrange the toasts on a platter and drizzle them with 1 tablespoon of the olive oil. Lay the slices of cheese on top of the tomato. Drizzle with the remaining tablespoon of olive oil and season to taste with sea salt.

In Catalonia, we love our toast, especially when it is topped with tomato and olive oil. Inspired by a Catalan classic, this snack is one part tradition and one part imagination.

José's Tip:

This slightly nutty cheese is amazing and will become a favorite in your home. It is easy to find online and in specialty markets. You could also substitute the more readily available Murcia al vino, or drunken goat cheese. Instead of using slices to make this tapa, I often grate the cheese over the toast, and I love to add anchovy fillets.

Pintxo Bonito con cebolla y tomate

Basque tapa of Bonito with soft onion and tomato

SERVES 4

4 TABLESPOONS SPANISH EXTRA-VIRGIN OLIVE OIL, PLUS MORE FOR DRIZZLING

½ LARGE ONION, THINLY SLICED

SEA SALT TO TASTE

8 ½-INCH BAGUETTE ROUNDS

2 RIPE PLUM TOMATOES

4 OUNCES SPANISH OIL-PACKED BONITO TUNA, SEPARATED INTO FLAKES

1 TABLESPOON CHOPPED CHIVES

Heat 3 tablespoons of the olive oil in a small sauté pan over low heat. Add the onion and cook slowly until golden brown, about 20 minutes. Add 1 tablespoon water if the onion starts to stick or burn. Season to taste with salt and cool to room temperature.

Toast the bread and set aside. Place a grater over a large mixing bowl. Halve the tomatoes and rub the cut surface of the tomatoes across the grater until all the flesh is grated. Discard the skin. Add the remaining tablespoon of olive oil to the grated tomato and season to taste with salt.

Spread the tomato pulp over the toasts. Place 1 tablespoon of the onions on top of each, then add 1 tablespoon of the tuna. Garnish with chives, drizzle with olive oil, and season to taste with sea salt.

There's nothing more appetizing than going into a bar in the Basque country and seeing a huge spread of colorful, complex pintxos. Just grab what you want from the bar and, as you savor each one, pick out the next. This pintxo is a great combination of crunchy toast, soft onion, and meaty Bonito tuna.

Pintxo Gilda

Basque tapa of olive, anchovy, and guindilla pepper

SERVES 4

8 GUINDILLA PEPPERS (PICKLED BASQUE PEPPERS) OR OTHER MILD LONG PICKLED PEPPERS

4 ANCHOVY FILLETS

8 PITTED MANZANILLA OLIVES (LARGE GREEN OLIVES ALSO KNOWN AS SPANISH OLIVES)

4 BOQUERONES (WHITE ANCHOVY FILLETS PACKED IN OIL AND VINEGAR)

Push a pepper three-quarters of the way onto a small skewer or large toothpick. Next, spear an anchovy and then an olive onto the skewer, pushing them close to the pepper. Repeat with 3 more peppers, anchovies, and olives. Then skewer the peppers, boquerónes, and olives in the same process.

This classic pintxo, with its burst of pepper, is named after the great Hollywood actress Rita Hayworth, whose starring role in the movie *Gilda* made a lasting impression on her Spanish fans during the Franco era.

José's Tip:
Each person should get one skewer with an anchovy and one with a boquerón. One of these skewers would be amazing in a martini!

Tortos de maiz con cebolla

Corn cakes with onions

Corn is not native to Spain, but it's been a highly successful transplant. Originally seen as something to feed the cows when wheat wasn't available, corn and corn flour were soon adopted by the Spanish people as a substitute for wheat. That's how we ended up with this kind of fried corn bread, which is to die for. Inspired by the tortos made by my friend Nacho Manzano at Casa Marcial, these are fluffy, light, and sweetened with onions.

SERVES 6 TO 8

FOR THE ONIONS

3 TABLESPOONS SPANISH EXTRA-VIRGIN OLIVE OIL

½ LARGE SPANISH ONION, THINLY SLICED

1 TEASPOON CIDER VINEGAR

FOR THE CORN CAKES

3 CUPS SPANISH EXTRA-VIRGIN OLIVE OIL

½ CUP FINE-GROUND CORN FLOUR

1 CUP ALL-PURPOSE FLOUR

½ TEASPOON BAKING POWDER

1 TEASPOON SALT

1 LARGE EGG

SEA SALT TO TASTE

1 TABLESPOON CHOPPED CHIVES

Prepare the onion: Heat the olive oil in a small sauté pan over low heat. Add the onion and slowly sauté until deep golden brown, about 45 minutes. Be sure to check the onion as it cooks; you may need to add 1 or 2 teaspoons water so it does not burn. Once the onion is deep brown, add the cider vinegar and cook until the vinegar evaporates. Remove the pan from the heat and season to taste with salt.

Prepare the corn cakes: Pour the olive oil into a pot and heat to 350°F (measured on a candy thermometer) over medium heat. Meanwhile, sift together the corn and all-purpose flours, the baking powder, and the teaspoon of salt in a mixing bowl. Add 5 ounces (about ⅔ cup) of warm water and mix well until the dough comes together and is sticky. Form the dough into a ball with your hands, then cover with a towel and let sit for 5 minutes. Cut the dough in half and then cut each half into 8 equal pieces. Roll each piece between the palms of your hands to make a ball. Place the ball of dough between 2 sheets of plastic wrap and press down with your fingers to create a disk about ⅛ inch thick. Peel off the plastic wrap, set aside, and cover with a damp towel. Repeat with the remaining dough until you have 16 rounds.

Working in batches so as not to crowd the pot, put the rounds into the hot oil and fry until golden brown on both sides and puffed, about 3 minutes. Transfer to a paper towel–lined plate to drain. Allow the oil to return to 350°F between batches.

Reheat the onions over medium-low heat, then remove from the heat and mix in the egg. The egg should be loose and not scrambled. Place the corn cakes on a plate, top with the egg-onion mixture, and season to taste with sea salt. Garnish with the chives.

José's Tip:

Make sure the oil stays at 350°F when frying the corn cakes. This will ensure that each batch turns out golden and crunchy.

Pimientos de Padrón con queso Tetilla

Padrón peppers with Tetilla cheese

SERVES 4 TO 6

24 FRESH PADRÓN PEPPERS

8 OUNCES TETILLA (SPANISH COW'S-MILK CHEESE FROM GALICIA), CUT INTO 1½ x ½-INCH-THICK STRIPS

2 TABLESPOONS SPANISH EXTRA-VIRGIN OLIVE OIL, PLUS MORE FOR DRIZZLING

SEA SALT TO TASTE

With a paring knife, make a slit down the center of each pepper from the top to the middle, being careful not to split them. Slide a strip of cheese into each slit and squeeze the pepper closed around it.

Heat 2 tablespoons olive oil in a small sauté pan or cast-iron griddle until hot and just smoking. Brown the peppers on each side, turning every 30 seconds, until the cheese melts. The peppers should keep some of their crunch, so do not let them cook for too long. Transfer the peppers to a plate, season with sea salt, and drizzle with olive oil before serving.

These special Galician ingredients are usually eaten on their own, but in this dish, we put them together for a perfect regional taste. The result is a warm combination of crunchy fresh pepper and creamy cheese. Most padrón peppers are mild and sweet, but every now and again you'll find a hot one. It's like Russian roulette on a plate.

José's Tip:
Padrón peppers are now being grown here in the United States. It's worth searching for them online and in specialty stores, along with the creamy Tetilla cheese. If you can't find them, mild serrano peppers and Monterey Jack cheese could be substituted.

Cerezas como aceitunas

Cherries as olives

SERVES 4

- 1 ORANGE
- 1 LEMON
- 5 GARLIC CLOVES
- 4 CUPS FRESH BING CHERRIES, STEMMED AND PITTED
- LEAVES FROM 4 FRESH ROSEMARY SPRIGS
- LEAVES FROM 6 FRESH THYME SPRIGS
- 1 BAY LEAF
- ½ CUP SPANISH EXTRA-VIRGIN OLIVE OIL
- ¼ CUP PEDRO XIMÉNEZ (PX) VINEGAR, OR SPANISH AGED SHERRY VINEGAR
- ¼ TEASPOON COARSE SEA SALT

Using a vegetable peeler, remove half of the zest from the orange and the lemon. Split the garlic cloves by placing them on a cutting board and pressing down hard with the flat side of a kitchen knife. Combine the garlic, cherries, lemon and orange zest, rosemary, thyme, bay leaf, olive oil, vinegar, and salt in a mixing bowl. Cover with plastic wrap and marinate for 4 hours at room temperature or overnight in the refrigerator. Allow refrigerated cherries to come to room temperature before serving.

José's Tip:
To add some crunch to these cherries, add 1 cup of Marcona almonds to the mix.

In Spain we love our marinated olives, but sometimes it's fun to play with the idea, changing an ingredient. Olives are just like cherries, don't you think? They are both rounded in shape, have stones at their core, and grow on trees. Here we use a savory marinade that is usually paired with olives to offset the sweet, juicy flesh of the cherries.

Anchoas con nectarinas

Nectarines with anchovies and Pedro Ximénez dressing

SERVES 4

1 TABLESPOON PEDRO XIMÉNEZ (PX) VINEGAR, OR SPANISH AGED SHERRY VINEGAR

3 TABLESPOONS SPANISH EXTRA-VIRGIN OLIVE OIL

SALT TO TASTE

2 RIPE NECTARINES

4 CUPS BABY MIXED GREENS

8 OIL-PACKED ANCHOVY FILLETS

½ TEASPOON CHOPPED CHIVES

Whisk the vinegar and olive oil together in a bowl and season to taste with salt.

Halve and pit the nectarines and cut them into ½-inch slices. Put the nectarine slices and the baby greens into another large mixing bowl and toss with 1 tablespoon of the dressing. Divide the salad among 4 plates and arrange 2 anchovy fillets on top of each serving. Drizzle with more dressing and garnish with chopped chives.

It's been my experience that behind almost every dish is a story. This dish's story is that it's the first tapa I conceived for my TV show in Spain. I don't recall if it was the first recipe we broadcast, but it was definitely the first that came into my head. It's a great tapa, and I especially love the way the acidity of the nectarines works with the saltiness of the anchovies.

José's Tip:

It is worth seeking out Pedro Ximénez vinegar. Chiefly grown in Montilla-Moriles, Málaga, and other parts of Andalusia, Pedro Ximénez is a white grape that was traditionally used to sweeten sherry. Today, it is better known as a dessert wine made from sun-dried grapes. Pedro Ximénez vinegar imparts a lovely sweet acidity to this recipe. If you cannot find Pedro Ximénez vinegar, try an aged sherry vinegar.

Aceitunas rellenas de anchoas y pimiento del piquillo

Stuffed olives with anchovies and piquillo peppers

SERVES 4

12 EXTRA-LARGE GREEN SPANISH OLIVES

6 OIL-PACKED ANCHOVY FILLETS

2 JARRED PIQUILLO PEPPERS

SPANISH EXTRA-VIRGIN OLIVE OIL

COARSE SEA SALT

1 ORANGE

Using the flat side of a knife, press down on each olive until the pit pops out, being careful not to split the olive in half. Cut the anchovy fillets lengthwise to create 12 long strips. Slice the peppers open and press them flat on a cutting board then cut the peppers into ¼-inch-wide strips

Stuff 1 piece of anchovy and 1 pepper strip into each olive. Place the olives on a platter, drizzle with olive oil, and sprinkle with salt. Use a microplane or zester to grate orange zest directly onto the stuffed olives.

Cantabria is known for its anchovies, which are of such high quality you really don't need to add much more to them than a great olive and a little pepper. These stuffed olives can be made hours before serving; just keep them marinating in olive oil until you are ready to serve.

José's Tip:
You can use pitted olives for this dish, but the olives will not have the same rich flavor.

Bocadillo de Despaña El Quixote

Sandwich of dried pork loin, Manchego cheese, and quince preserve

SERVES 4

8 SLICES RUSTIC BREAD

SPANISH EXTRA-VIRGIN OLIVE OIL

1 BLOCK MEMBRILLO (QUINCE PRESERVE), ABOUT 12 OUNCES, CUT INTO ¼-INCH SLICES

½ POUND THINLY SLICED LOMO EMBUCHADO (DRIED CURED PORK LOIN)

½ POUND THINLY SLICED MANCHEGO (SPANISH SHEEP'S-MILK CHEESE)

Toast or grill the slices of bread and drizzle each slice with olive oil. Top 4 slices of the bread with the sliced membrillo, followed by slices of pork loin, then slices of the Manchego. Drizzle the Manchego with more olive oil and top each sandwich with a second slice of grilled bread.

José's Tip:

The finest membrillo, like the Santa Teresa brand in Spain, is often found in blocks and is easy to slice. You can also use membrillo that comes in a small tub; instead of slicing it, spread it on each piece of bread. If you cannot find cured pork loin, use Serrano ham.

Despaña is a wonderful gourmet shop on New York's Lower East Side that carries all sorts of imported Spanish foods and also offers prepared food to take out. To find a place like this in New York fills me with joy; it reminds me of the little shops in Spain that make sandwiches to order with whatever ingredients you choose. My friends Angélica and Marcos Intriago do a superb job with the sandwiches in their store, and this is one of my favorites.

Bocadillo de calamares fritos con allioli

Squid sandwich with garlic mayonnaise

SERVES 4

3 TABLESPOONS SPANISH EXTRA-VIRGIN OLIVE OIL

½ LARGE ONION, THINLY SLICED

SEA SALT TO TASTE

4 6-INCH-LONG SANDWICH ROLLS

1 POUND FRESH SMALL SQUID, BODIES AND TENTACLES SEPARATED

4 CUPS OLIVE OIL

2 CUPS ALL-PURPOSE FLOUR

4 TABLESPOONS ALLIOLI (PAGE 250)

Heat 3 tablespoons of olive oil in a small sauté pan over low heat. Add the onion and cook slowly until golden brown, about 20 minutes. Add 1 tablespoon water if the onion starts to stick or burn. Season to taste with salt and cool to room temperature. Preheat oven to 350°F.

Slice open the rolls, being careful not to cut all the way through. Lay them open on a baking sheet and toast lightly.

With a sharp knife, cut the squid bodies into 1-inch rings.

Heat 4 cups of olive oil in a deep pot over medium heat until it measures 350°F on a candy thermometer. Put the flour in a large mixing bowl and season with salt. Add the squid rings and tentacles and coat with the flour. Drop the floured squid into a mesh strainer or colander and shake gently to knock off any excess flour. Working in batches, fry the squid in the hot oil until golden, about 45 seconds. Transfer to a paper towel-lined plate with a slotted spoon and drain. Allow the oil to return to 350°F between batches.

Spread ½ tablespoon of allioli on each side of the toasted rolls. Spoon the caramelized onions on one side of each roll. Fill each roll with fried squid and serve immediately.

José's Tip:
By toasting the rolls to a nice brown color, you'll give these sandwiches even more crunch.

This sandwich is a Madrid classic around the Plaza Mayor, but I ate my first squid sandwich in the town of San Fernando in the southern province of Cadíz, where I was doing my military service in the navy. I always looked forward to a fried squid sandwich when they gave us a day off. Beer is the usual accompaniment, but I'm not a beer drinker, so I always enjoyed my sandwich with a good sherry, which is quite traditional in Cadíz. I still think it's the best chaser for this exquisite sandwich.

Melón y jamón

Ribbons of melon and ham

SERVES 4

4 OUNCES THINLY SLICED JAMÓN SERRANO (SPANISH CURED HAM)

3 TABLESPOONS SPANISH EXTRA-VIRGIN OLIVE OIL

1 TABLESPOON SHERRY VINEGAR

SEA SALT TO TASTE

4 OUNCES CANTALOUPE, THINLY SLICED

1 TABLESPOON MINCED CHIVES

Preheat the oven to 350°F. Line a baking sheet with parchment paper. Arrange 2 ounces of the jamón on the prepared baking sheet. Roast in the oven for 10 minutes or until crisp, then set aside to cool. Once cool enough to handle, crumble the jamón with your fingers.

Whisk the olive oil and sherry vinegar together in a mixing bowl and season to taste with salt. Drape alternating slices of melon and the remaining jamón on each plate like loose ribbons. Drizzle some dressing on top and garnish with chives and the crumbled crispy jamón.

José's Tip:
Choose a melon that is ripe but not so ripe that you cannot slice it thinly into ribbons.

Walk through any traditional market in Spain, and you will find the makings of great snacks. While I was filming in the Chamartín market in Madrid, I just couldn't resist a display of the special melons we call *Villaconejos*. These melons, to me, are the best in the world. Pair them with a slice of Ibérico ham, and you have a wonderful tapa. This recipe celebrates the great markets of the world, where experts behind every counter treat the food as if they had produced it themselves. Markets in Spain have been run this way for generations; I hope they'll continue to thrive for many more.

In Spanish cooking, vegetables are much more than a side dish or mere accompaniment to meat or fish. Fresh vegetables are highly valued by Spanish cooks—to the point where we prize certain varieties over others and showcase them in dishes on their own. Sometimes vegetables have been elevated to greatness in recipes by working people who could not afford meat; other times the vegetables are stars in their own right thanks to their special qualities, like the sweet piquillo peppers from the region of Navarre. Vegetable dishes connect us to the land and our environment, whether they come from our own gardens or the fertile river plains of the north. One of the best chefs in Spain is my friend Andoni Luis Aduriz, who spends almost as much time in his vegetable garden as he does in his kitchen, close to San Sebastián. His astonishingly varied work with herbs, greens, and plant shoots shows just how complex and subtle Spanish vegetable dishes can be.

vegetables

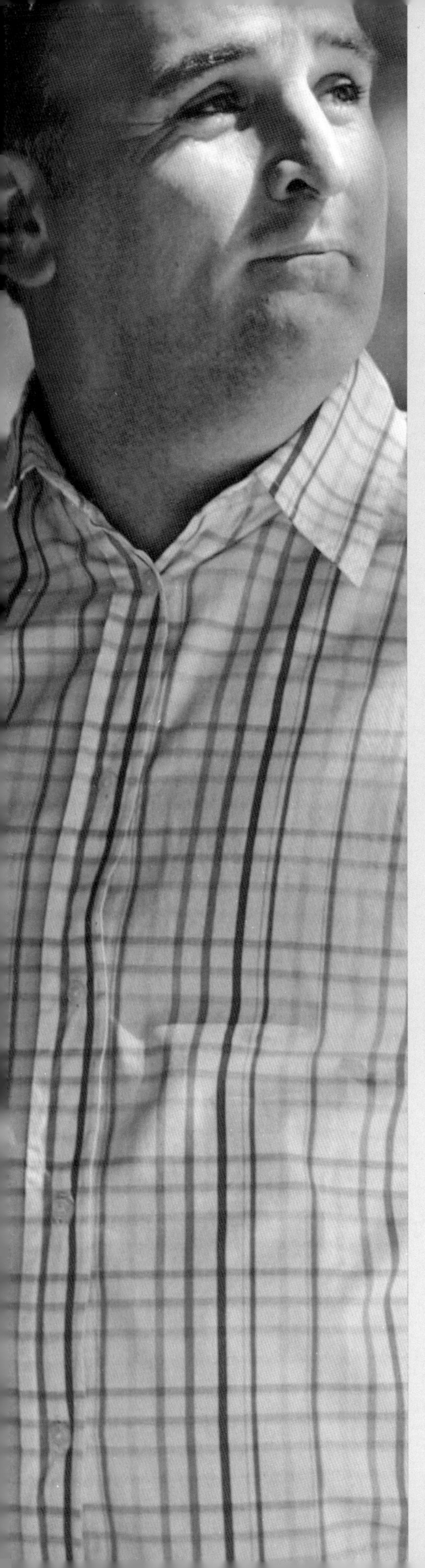

navarra

Navarre, a region south of the Basque country, was immortalized in Ernest Hemingway's account of the famous running of the bulls in Pamplona. Every July, during the festival of Sanfermines, six bulls are freed to run through the city's narrow streets, a spectacle that transfixes the nation and much of the rest of the world. What really fascinates me, though, are some of the nameless buildings that line the bulls' route. Here you can find the gastronomic societies or clubs where men gather to improve their cooking skills and share culinary knowledge. They also prepare the famous bull-meat stews that are served after the bull run.

Navarre is a great gastronomic region with a rich history. It was home to an Augustine monk from Pamplona called Antonio Salsete who, in the late seventeenth century, wrote the masterpiece *El Cocinero Religioso* (*The Monastic Cook*). Navarre has long been a region of wild boars, partridge, and wood pigeon. Its rivers were traditionally full of trout, and those same rivers helped to create some of the best farming land in Spain. The white asparagus of Navarre is such a wonder that, when it is in season, the local restaurants take part in a festival celebrating its arrival. The region's most famous vegetable, though, is the piquillo pepper, a deep red, hand-roasted pepper whose newfound popularity is helping spread the name of Navarre around the world.

My good friend Ricardo Guelbenzu owns a winery in the region and exemplifies the spirit of Navarre. He loves food and wine and is welcoming to friends and foreigners alike. That love of life makes you wonder why anyone would ever leave Navarre. If you make it to the region's capital, Logroño, be sure to visit their great tapas street, called Laurel. There you'll find the people of Navarre enjoying their favorite activity: celebrating life—and delicious food—with friends.

OFERTA
3 BOTES
9E
Muy
LODOSILLA
PIMIENTOS
del piquillo
Rioja
CALIDAD
Loza
RIOJA
CALIDAD
RONCAL
RONKARI
11 €

Migas con níscalos y jamón

Bread with oyster mushrooms and Spanish ham

SERVES 4

5 TABLESPOONS SPANISH EXTRA-VIRGIN OLIVE OIL

2 CUPS THINLY SLICED DAY-OLD BAGUETTE

1 TABLESPOON MINCED SHALLOT

1 MEDIUM BANANA PEPPER, STEMMED, SEEDED, AND SLICED

2 CUPS OYSTER MUSHROOMS OR SAFFRON MILK CAP MUSHROOMS (AVAILABLE IN AUTUMN)

2 FRESH THYME SPRIGS

2 OUNCES THINLY SLICED JAMÓN SERRANO (SPANISH CURED HAM)

¼ CUP SEEDLESS RED GRAPES, HALVED

SEA SALT TO TASTE

Heat 2 tablespoons of the olive oil in a large sauté pan over medium heat. Working in batches, sauté the bread slices until golden, 8 to 10 minutes. Add another tablespoon of olive oil if needed. Transfer the bread to a bowl and set aside.

Heat the remaining 2 tablespoons of the olive oil in the same pan over medium heat. Add the shallot and cook until translucent, about 1 minute. Add the pepper and cook until soft, about 3 minutes. Add the mushrooms and the thyme and cook, stirring, for 3 minutes. Add the jamón and cook for 1 minute. Stir the fried bread into the mixture and continue to cook until well combined. Stir in the grapes and season to taste with salt.

José's Tip:
Use day-old bread for this dish. You will get a better crunch.

There are several versions of migas, a dish that has sustained many a Spanish family when food was scarce. I often talk about recipes made of humble ingredients that can feed an entire family, and this is a perfect example. It shows what can be done when leftovers are the only option. Over the years, many of these survival dishes have become beloved delicacies. I love this one for its simplicity and intense flavor.

Tumbet Mallorquín

Roasted vegetables, Mallorca style

SERVES 4

4 PLUM TOMATOES

1 CUP SPANISH EXTRA-VIRGIN OLIVE OIL

2 MEDIUM GLOBE EGGPLANTS, CUT INTO ¼-INCH SLICES

4 RUSSET POTATOES, PEELED AND CUT INTO ¼-INCH SLICES

2 RED BELL PEPPERS, SEEDED AND CUT INTO 1-INCH STRIPS

2 GREEN BELL PEPPERS, SEEDED AND CUT INTO 1-INCH STRIPS

SEA SALT

1 BUNCH OF FRESH THYME SPRIGS

1 BUNCH OF FRESH ROSEMARY SPRIGS

4 GARLIC CLOVES, PEELED

Slice the tomatoes in half. Place a grater over a mixing bowl. Rub the cut surface of the tomatoes over the grater until all of the flesh is grated. Discard the skins and set the grated tomatoes aside.

Preheat the oven to 375°F.

Heat ¾ cup of the olive oil in a large sauté pan over medium-high heat. Working in batches, sauté the eggplant, potatoes, and peppers for 1 minute on each side. Place a single layer of potatoes on the bottom of a 1½-quart baking dish, season with salt, and top with a large spoonful of grated tomato, 2 sprigs of thyme, and 2 sprigs of rosemary. Next, arrange a single layer of eggplant, season with salt, and top with grated tomato and herbs. Add a layer of the peppers, season with salt, and top with grated tomato and herbs. Continue layering the vegetables, grated tomato, and herbs until all the ingredients are used for a total of about 10 layers.

Split open the garlic cloves by pressing down on each with the flat side of a kitchen knife. Tuck the crushed garlic into the layers of the vegetables and drizzle with the remaining ¼ cup of olive oil. Bake for 30 minutes. Serve immediately.

José's Tip:
After each layer of vegetables, press down lightly with your fingers to compact them. This will make it easier to slice and serve after baking.

When I was twelve or thirteen years old, I went to summer camp in the beautiful islands of Mallorca. The cook made this traditional mix of vegetables, layered in slices, and I thought it was wonderful. After eating every bit of my own serving, I would always ask my friends to give me their plates if they didn't finish.

Patatas Arrugadas

Wrinkled potatoes, Canary Island style

SERVES 4

2 POUNDS BABY POTATOES

1 CUP SALT, PLUS MORE AS NEEDED

MOJO ROJO OR MOJO VERDE (PAGE 244), FOR DIPPING

Put the potatoes in a medium deep pot. Cover with water and add 1 cup of salt. You need enough salt in the water to cause the potatoes to float, so add more if needed. Bring to a boil over high heat, then reduce the heat to a simmer and cook the potatoes for 25 to 30 minutes. Use a toothpick to check for doneness. The potatoes will start to wrinkle as they get tender.

Pour out most of the water, leaving just enough to cover the bottom of the pot, and return the pot to the stovetop. Shake the pot over the low heat until the salt covering the potatoes begins to crystallize, about 5 minutes. Take the potatoes off the heat and cover with a clean kitchen towel until the potato skins have wrinkled, about 10 minutes. Serve the potatoes with mojo sauces.

This dish is inspired by the delicious potatoes grown in the Canary Islands, which are off the coast of Africa. The islands were historically the last port between Spain and the Americas, and with their tropical climate, they became home to many American products. Although the potatoes on the islands are especially wonderful, you can re-create this dish with the flavorful varieties that grow in America. If you want the real thing, though, fly to the islands. It's well worth the trip.

Alcachofas rellenas de huevos de cordoniz y huevas de trucha

Artichokes stuffed with quail egg and trout roe

SERVES 4

8 BABY ARTICHOKES

1 BUNCH FRESH PARSLEY

8 QUAIL EGGS

SEA SALT TO TASTE

2 OUNCES TROUT ROE

¼ CUP SPANISH EXTRA-VIRGIN OLIVE OIL

1 TABLESPOON FINELY CHOPPED PARSLEY

José's Tip:
Mini muffin tins can be a great help when making these artichokes. Place the artichoke bottoms in the muffin cups, top with the quail eggs, and bake. Then you won't have to worry about any of the artichokes tipping over. You can also top the artichokes with salmon roe.

Use a serrated knife to cut off the top half of each artichoke. Break off and discard all of the exterior leaves until you reach the pale green, tender center leaves. Pry open the leaves with your fingers and use a spoon to scrape out the white, hairy interior (choke). Use a small knife to peel away the tough outer layer around the base of the artichoke until you reach the soft white flesh. Cut off the stems to give each artichoke a flat bottom. As you work, put the trimmed artichokes into a large bowl of cold water and add the parsley to stop them from oxidizing and coloring.

Place the artichokes in a medium pot with water to cover and boil until tender, about 5 minutes. Transfer the artichokes to a large bowl filled with ice water. Once cooled, drain the artichokes and lay on paper towels to dry.

Preheat the oven to 350°F.

Gently crack a quail egg with a small knife and slide the egg into a small cup or bowl. Sprinkle some salt around the egg white (this will help the egg cook evenly). Using a small spoon, gently transfer the egg to an artichoke bottom. Repeat with the remaining eggs and artichoke bottoms.

Place the egg-filled artichokes on a sheet pan (see tip) and bake for 3 minutes, or until the egg is slightly set. Transfer the artichokes to a platter and garnish each with a small spoonful of the trout roe. Drizzle with the olive oil and sprinkle sea salt around the platter.

With all the creativity in Spanish cooking over the last fifteen or twenty years, you can now eat great new dishes at bars as well as high-end restaurants. This dish, created by my friend Dídac López Amat at La Estrella de Plata, is one of my favorites. Sadly, the restaurant has now closed, but it proved you don't have to run a luxurious place to serve delicious, creative food.

Fabada Asturiana

Asturian bean stew

SERVES 4 TO 6

½ POUND FABES (LARGE DRIED WHITE BEANS FROM ASTURIAS)

¼ POUND SMOKED BACON SLAB

4 CUPS CHICKEN STOCK

1 HEAD GARLIC, PAPERY OUTER SKIN REMOVED

2 MEDIUM SPANISH ONIONS, 1 HALVED AND 1 MINCED

1 3-POUND CHICKEN, CUT INTO PIECES

¼ CUP SPANISH EXTRA-VIRGIN OLIVE OIL

1 TEASPOON SWEET PIMENTÓN (SPANISH SMOKED PAPRIKA)

PINCH OF SAFFRON, THREADS CRUSHED

José's Tip:
If you can't find fabes, use another large dried white bean, like gigantes. Note that the beans must soak overnight.

The day before you plan to cook the stew, place the beans in a bowl and cover with cold water. Soak the beans overnight at room temperature. The next day, drain and rinse the beans.

Put the bacon slab in a small pot, cover with water, and boil for 5 minutes. Drain the bacon. (This will remove some of the fat.)

Combine the drained beans and chicken stock in a large pot. Remove 1 garlic clove from the head and set aside. Add the bacon, the head of garlic, and the halved onion. Bring to a slow boil, skimming any foam that rises to the top. Simmer for 15 minutes, then add the chicken pieces.

Meanwhile, in a medium sauté pan, heat the olive oil over medium heat. Add the minced onion and cook until it is translucent and begins to caramelize, about 15 minutes. Peel and mince the reserved clove of garlic and add it to the onion. Cook for 2 more minutes, then stir in the pimentón and saffron. Spoon the onion mixture into the large pot and stir until well combined.

Continue to cook the beans and chicken, uncovered, at a very low simmer for 2 hours. Occasionally add a little cold water to slow the simmering and to keep the beans covered with liquid. (Do not stir the beans while they cook; this could cause them to break apart.) Remove the pot from the heat, cover, and set aside to cool for 1 hour. Remove and discard the onion halves and head of garlic. Remove the bacon and cut into thin slices.

Ladle the beans and chicken pieces into soup bowls and garnish with slices of the bacon.

This version of the classic Asturian stew was adapted by a young chef who triumphed against all odds by opening a restaurant in the house where he was born—in a beautiful mountain setting, close to where his mother and grandmother live. Nacho Manzano's Casa Marcial is where tradition and modernity meet. He uses produce grown by him or by farmers living in the same community. As you eat this stew, maybe on a cold and rainy day, you may find yourself transported to the days when the miners and shepherds would go home and eat this hearty dish to recover from their labors.

Judías negras de Tolosa

Tolosa black beans

SERVES 4

2 CUPS TOLOSA BEANS (BLACK BEANS FROM THE BASQUE COUNTRY)

1 BAY LEAF

4 TABLESPOONS SPANISH EXTRA-VIRGIN OLIVE OIL

1 POUND PORK SPARE RIBS, SEPARATED

¼ POUND SMOKED BACON

1 MEDIUM SPANISH ONION, MINCED

4 GARLIC CLOVES, MINCED

½ HEAD SAVOY CABBAGE, CUT IN HALF AND LEAVES SEPARATED

SEA SALT TO TASTE

The day before you plan to cook the stew, place the beans in a bowl and cover with cold water. Soak the beans overnight at room temperature. The next day, drain and rinse the beans.

Put the beans and bay leaf into a medium pot, cover with water, and bring to a boil over medium-high heat. Once foam appears, remove the pot from the heat and skim off the foam.

Heat the olive oil in a large pot or casserole dish over medium-high heat. Add the ribs and cook until browned on both sides. Add the bacon and onion, and cook, stirring, for 3 minutes. Add the garlic and sauté until golden, about 5 minutes. Add the drained beans and enough water to cover the meat and beans. Reduce the heat to low, cover, and simmer for 1 hour, stirring occasionally, until the beans are tender and cooked through.

Add the cabbage leaves and continue to cook for 30 minutes. Season to taste with salt. Discard the bay leaf. To serve, remove the bacon, ribs, and cabbage from the pot and cut into small pieces. Divide the beans among shallow soup bowls and serve the meats and cabbage on small side plates.

José's Tip:

Do not stir the beans as they cook. They may break apart, and you want these beans to stay nice and round. You can use black turtle beans if you cannot find the Tolosa variety. Note that the beans must soak overnight.

I find these beans fascinating; each one looks as if it has been polished by hand. It's impossible to make a bad dish with them, and they are well worth the effort of finding them. If you can't, buy two tickets to Tolosa with the love of your life. He or she will love you forever.

Until well into the twentieth century, most of Spain's cheeses were known only in their own regions. Transport and communications were difficult in many of the best cheesemaking areas, where local artisans had developed their own cheeses based on centuries of tradition. Locally bred herds, grazing on ancient pastures, produced special milk that in turn yielded distinctive cheeses. Sometimes the cheesemaking technique reflected the region's unique geographical features, as in Asturias, where the caves are perfect for cultivating the mold inside blue cheeses. Sometimes the technique reflected the lifestyle of shepherds, living in small huts with open fires that gave a smoky aroma to their cheese. It was only in the 1960s and 1970s that people started to document and catalog the wide variety of Spain's regional cheeses. That process helped preserve and popularize some extraordinary cheesemaking, such as the village cheeses of Cantabria or the fabulously runny torta cheeses of Extremadura. By the 1980s, new cheesemakers emerged, reviving old products and inventing new ones. As Spanish cheeses have become more famous, they have become more widely available. Now we can enjoy the great cheeses of Spain across the world—and cook uniquely Spanish dishes in our own homes.

cheese and eggs

Emilia
Anguletas
Conservas
Emilia
Emilia
Anguletas
Emilia
Anguletas
Emilia
BONANA
1'75
REDONDA
3.50 €/kg
2.50 €/k
SOJA
3.50 €/kg
CARICOS

cantabria

I made my first semi-adult trip to Cantabria on the occasion of my grandmother's death. Although it was a sad time, it was also a magical moment of gastronomic awakening for me. My relatives lived in the Santander area, close to the capital of Cantabria, in a town called El Sardinero—the place of the sardines. There I made a fascinating series of food discoveries, one after another. Among those were sobados, a traditional Cantabrian sweet made from butter and eggs with a fluffy texture, a bit like madeleines but made in squares. They taste even better when they are dipped in milk from the great Cantabrian cows, found all across the region. Cantabria is famous for its dairy products, including the wonderful little artisanal cheeses they call *Quesucos de Liébana.* And I can't forget the best ice cream I ever ate, bought in a tiny shop, where it was made fresh every morning using only natural flavors. The milk was unpasteurized, which added to the creaminess.

But the highlight of that visit was the trip I took to Pedreña, across the bay from the port of Santander. Pedreña is famous for many things, not least as the place where the young Severiano Ballesteros played golf before he became one of the best players in the world. But for me, it was all about the sardines. I went to one of the small informal beach bars they call *chiringuitos.* The main dish they offered was sardines grilled over charcoal, served with a simple but refreshing salad of tomatoes, onions, and romaine lettuce—a salad beloved throughout Spain. I had enjoyed sardines many times before, but somehow these sardines, which had just been caught off the coast of Santander, were transcendent. They were big and plump and fatty and smoky with the aroma of the charcoal. I lost track of how many I ate. I just watched as the trays kept coming to my table.

Huevo frito con chorizo

Fried egg with chorizo

SERVES 4

8 GARLIC CLOVES, PEELED

¼ CUP SPANISH EXTRA-VIRGIN OLIVE OIL, PLUS 1 TABLESPOON

4 LARGE EGGS

SEA SALT TO TASTE

1 LINK CHORIZO, ABOUT 4 OUNCES, SLICED INTO ¼-INCH ROUNDS

4 FRESH THYME SPRIGS

José's Tip:
Use the freshest eggs you can find for this dish. Get them from a farmers' market if you can.

Split the garlic cloves by pressing down on them with the flat side of a kitchen knife. Heat 1 tablespoon of the olive oil in a medium sauté pan over medium heat. Add the garlic and cook until lightly browned, about 5 minutes. Transfer the garlic to a plate and set aside.

Increase the heat under the pan to medium-high and add the remaining ¼ cup of olive oil. Cook the eggs one at a time. For each, crack the egg into a glass. When the oil just begins to smoke, tip the sauté pan to a steep angle so the oil collects on one side to create a small bath. Carefully slide the egg into the hot oil and spoon the hot oil over the egg 2 or 3 times. The egg will be ready in about 30 seconds. Transfer the egg to a serving plate with a slotted spoon, season to taste with salt, and keep warm. Repeat with the remaining eggs.

Pour the olive oil from the pan into a small bowl and set aside. Return the pan to the stovetop. Add the chorizo and cook for 30 to 45 seconds over medium-high heat, flipping the rounds when they begin to brown. Add the thyme and continue cooking for 1 minute.

To serve, divide the chorizo and thyme among 4 plates, top each with an egg, and garnish with the reserved garlic. Sprinkle with sea salt and drizzle the reserved cooking oil over each plate.

I'm fascinated by eggs and have been since I was a little boy. On a trip to Barcelona with my friend the food writer Gael Greene, she was fascinated to see we ate eggs everywhere we went. I especially love fried eggs: the crispiness of the edges of the whites combined with the soft, runny texture of the yolks. All you need to do is sprinkle on some coarse salt, dip in a bit of bread, and you're in heaven. Or Spain.

Queso Cabrales con manzanas y aceite de oliva

Cabrales blue cheese with apples and olive oil

SERVES 4

- 1 TABLESPOON CIDER VINEGAR, PREFERABLY SPANISH
- 3 TABLESPOONS SPANISH EXTRA-VIRGIN OLIVE OIL
- SEA SALT AND FRESHLY CRACKED BLACK PEPPER TO TASTE
- 2 GRANNY SMITH APPLES
- 2 OUNCES CABRALES (SPANISH BLUE CHEESE)
- 1 TEASPOON CHOPPED CHIVES
- ¼ CUP MARCONA ALMONDS
- SEA SALT TO TASTE

Prepare the dressing: Whisk together the vinegar and olive oil in a mixing bowl and season to taste with salt and pepper.

Core the apples with an apple corer. Using a mandoline, thinly slice 1 of the apples into rings. Cut the remaining apple into ¼-inch-thick sticks. Divide the rings and sticks among 4 plates. Crumble the cheese on top of each plate and sprinkle with chives. Grate the almonds over the apples with a microplane or chop them finely with a knife and sprinkle on top. Drizzle with dressing and season to taste with salt.

José's Tip:
You can use a good local blue cheese or a Stilton if you can't find Cabrales.

I don't know whether God put Cabrales cheese on Earth to be a companion for apples or if apples were created to add sweetness to the Cabrales. What I do know is that one supports the other, and that both ingredients are vital to the cooking of my home region, Asturias.

Tostada de La Serena con mermelada

La Serena toast with lemon marmalade

SERVES 4

1 2-POUND WHEEL OF LA SERENA

1 LEMON

1 CUP SUGAR

1 LOAF OF BRIOCHE OR WHITE BREAD

SPANISH EXTRA-VIRGIN OLIVE OIL

Using a sharp kitchen knife, slice off the top of the cheese (where the label lies). Set on a platter and allow the cheese to rest at room temperature for 3 hours. The cheese should be soft enough to scoop with a spoon.

Meanwhile, use a vegetable peeler to remove the zest from the lemon. Slice the zest into thin strips. Slice off the top and bottom of the lemon. Stand the lemon on a cutting board and, using a kitchen knife, cut off all the pith in long, straight cuts. Slice the lemon in half lengthwise and chop it into small pieces. Put the strips of lemon zest, the chopped lemon pulp, and the sugar in a small pot with 1 cup water. Bring to a simmer, then reduce the heat to very low and cook for 45 minutes to 1 hour at a low simmer. Do not allow the mixture to boil. Once the mixture has reduced to a thick marmalade consistency, set aside to cool.

Preheat the oven to 400°F.

Trim the bread into 8 logs, 1½ x 1 x 3 inches. Using a small melon baller or paring knife, carefully scoop out a 2-inch-long channel from the top of each log. Toast the logs on a baking sheet for 2 to 3 minutes per side, turning them, or until golden brown. Fill the channel with spoonfuls of cheese, enough to reach the top of the toast, then top with a spoonful of the marmalade. Arrange the toasts on a platter and drizzle olive oil across them before serving.

Any serious food tourist in Spain should take the trouble to go to Extremadura to eat the special cheese we call *tortas*. All you have to do is toast some bread and dip it into the runny heart of this magical cheese. It's unbelievably addictive.

José's Tip:

Freezing the bread makes it easier to cut out the channel. You can also cut it out by using a sharp paring knife to make a horizontal slit about ¼ inch from the bottom of the log, being careful not to cut through the other sides. Then take the knife and insert it into the top of the log down to where the horizontal slit is and cut around the center channel. The bread should pop out easily.

Manchego con tomate

Manchego with tomato, thyme, and walnuts

SERVES 4

1/4 CUP WHOLE WALNUTS

2 RIPE PLUM TOMATOES

2 TABLESPOONS SPANISH EXTRA-VIRGIN OLIVE OIL

SEA SALT AND FRESHLY CRACKED BLACK PEPPER TO TASTE

2 FRESH ROSEMARY SPRIGS

8 OUNCES MANCHEGO (SPANISH SHEEP'S-MILK CHEESE), CUT INTO 1/2-INCH CUBES

Preheat the oven to 350°F. Spread the walnuts on a baking sheet. Toast them in the oven for 5 minutes.

Slice the tomatoes in half. Place a grater over a mixing bowl. Rub the cut surface of the tomatoes over the grater until all of the flesh is grated. Discard the skins.

Add the olive oil and walnuts to the tomato pulp. Stir and season to taste with salt and pepper. Strip the leaves from the rosemary sprigs and add to the tomato mixture, then toss in the cheese. To serve, spoon some of the mixture onto a serving plate and spear the cheese cubes with toothpicks.

I love hard cheese marinated in olive oil, herbs, and citrus. I also love the Catalan classic tapa of tomato bread topped with Manchego cheese. One day I got inspired and decided to try something new. I left out the bread and marinated the cheese with olive oil and tomato. I think you'll find it's a great combination.

José's Tip:

Serve this dish within hours of making it. If you let the cheese sit too long in the tomato pulp, the acid from the tomato will begin to soften it.

Tortilla de "montgetes" y cebolla tierna

Omelet with white beans and green onions

SERVES 4

½ CUP DRIED WHITE BEANS (NAVY BEANS)

1 HEAD GARLIC, PAPERY SKIN REMOVED, HALVED HORIZONTALLY

1 BAY LEAF

5 TABLESPOONS SPANISH EXTRA-VIRGIN OLIVE OIL

½ CUP THINLY SLICED SCALLIONS (GREEN PARTS ONLY)

8 LARGE EGGS

1 TABLESPOON CHOPPED FRESH PARSLEY

SEA SALT TO TASTE

José's Tip:
This is an open-face tortilla where the eggs should be a bit runny. If you'd like the eggs cooked through, flip the tortilla and cook for 30 seconds more. Note the beans require presoaking.

The day before you plan to cook the tortilla, place the beans in a bowl and cover with cold water. Set aside to soak overnight at room temperature. The next day, drain and rinse the beans.

Put the beans in a pot, add 1½ quarts of water, the garlic, bay leaf, and 2 tablespoons of the olive oil and bring to a boil over medium-high heat. Reduce the heat to a low simmer for 1 hour or until the beans are tender. Drain the beans, discard the garlic and bay leaf, and set aside.

Working in batches, heat 1 tablespoon of the olive oil in a sauté pan over medium heat. Spread half of the white beans in one layer and cook until lightly browned on one side, about 3 minutes. Add half of the scallions and sauté for 1 minute. Repeat with the remaining beans and scallions, adding another tablespoon of oil if necessary. Set the beans aside and keep warm.

Heat ½ tablespoon of the olive oil in a 6-inch nonstick sauté pan over medium heat. Lightly whisk the eggs in a bowl then pour one-quarter of the eggs into the sauté pan. Run a spatula around the edge of the eggs and shake the pan vigorously to prevent the tortilla from sticking to the pan. Spread one-quarter of the beans across the eggs and cook until the eggs are just set. The tortilla should remain a little runny in the center. Slide the tortilla onto a warm plate, garnish with parsley, and add salt to taste. Repeat with the remaining eggs and beans, adding more olive oil to the pan when needed (you should have 4 tortillas).

In Catalonia we love our eggs, especially in the form of tortillas, or omelets. We make tortillas with everything and anything, including dried beans, as in this hearty version. If you can find the Catalan beans called *montgetes*, you'll see how extraordinary beans and eggs can be; if not, navy beans will get you close to heaven.

Tortilla de sobrasada y queso Mahón

Omelet of Mallorquín sausage and Mahón cheese

SERVES 4

8 LARGE EGGS

4 OUNCES MAHÓN (SPANISH COW'S-MILK CHEESE FROM MENORCA), DICED

SEA SALT TO TASTE

4 1-OUNCE SLICES OF SOBRASADA SAUSAGE

4 TEASPOONS SPANISH EXTRA-VIRGIN OLIVE OIL

Break 2 eggs into a mixing bowl and whisk them vigorously. Stir in one-quarter of the cheese and season to taste with salt.

Heat a 6-inch sauté pan over medium heat. Once the pan is hot, lay 1 slice of the sobrasada in the pan and cook for 2 minutes on each side, then set aside on a warm plate. Quickly wipe the sauté pan with a paper towel and return it to the stovetop on medium heat. Lay the browned slice of sobrasada in the center of the pan and pour the whisked eggs and cheese over the sausage.

Run a spatula around the edge of the eggs and shake the pan vigorously for 10 to 15 seconds to prevent the tortilla from sticking. Flip the tortilla when the edges are cooked but the center has not set. Place a plate over the pan and invert the pan and plate together so the tortilla ends up on the plate, uncooked side down. Add 1 teaspoon of the olive oil to the pan and slide the tortilla back into the pan, uncooked side down. Continue cooking for another 30 seconds. Transfer the tortilla to a serving plate and keep warm. Repeat with the remaining ingredients to form 3 more tortillas. Serve immediately.

We started serving this dish in my restaurant Jaleo around four or five years ago, with this simple description: two great ingredients from the Balearic Islands. All we did was combine eggs with the beautiful, smoky flavor of sobrasada sausage and sweet, creamy Mahón cheese. It's one of the most successful omelets we ever created.

José's Tip:

If you don't feel comfortable flipping the tortilla, set it under the broiler to finish cooking the egg. Sobrasada sausage and Mahón cheese are readily available at specialty markets and online. It's important to use sobrasada in this recipe because it gives the right amount of fatty flavor that melts into the cheese and eggs.

Tortilla de patatas

Potato omelet

SERVES 4

3 CUPS PLUS 2 TABLESPOONS SPANISH EXTRA-VIRGIN OLIVE OIL

½ POUND RUSSET POTATOES, PEELED, QUARTERED, AND THINLY SLICED

6 LARGE EGGS

1 TEASPOON SEA SALT

Heat 3 cups of the olive oil in a medium pot over medium-low heat until it measures 250°F on a candy thermometer. Fry the potatoes until golden brown, about 20 minutes. With a slotted spoon, transfer the potatoes to paper towels to drain.

Using an electric mixer, beat the eggs in a large bowl with the salt. You want them to incorporate a lot of air so they fluff up. Add the cooked potatoes to the beaten eggs and let sit for 1 minute.

Heat the remaining 2 tablespoons olive oil in a 12-inch sauté pan over high heat. Once the oil begins to smoke slightly, remove the pan from the heat and pour in the egg-potato mixture. Return the sauté pan to the stovetop and reduce the heat to low. The tortilla will puff up like a soufflé. Once it begins to set and the edges turn golden brown, flip the tortilla. Place a plate over the pan and invert the pan and plate together so the tortilla ends up on the plate, uncooked side down. Slide the tortilla back into the pan, uncooked side down.

Make a small hole in the center of the tortilla to allow the egg in the center to cook. Once the tortilla sets, flip the tortilla back over and allow the center hole to close. Transfer the tortilla to a platter, cut into wedges, and serve.

I have read a great deal about the Galician restaurant El Manjar over the years, but I never got the chance to eat there until recently. I was amazed at how they make their tortilla with a few simple ingredients: eggs, potatoes, olive oil, and salt. It might look easy to cook an omelet, but it takes a lot of practice to cook omelets as well as they do at El Manjar. This recipe is inspired by theirs—and it's well worth the effort to master.

extremadura

I don't know about you, but my wife and I don't plan vacations thinking about what museums and monuments we want to visit. We plan them around the restaurants and wineries we want to try and the local delicacies we want to eat. As a general rule, I've found that if a place has something worth eating, then it will have some building or other attraction worth seeing as well. Extremadura is just such a place. It's a semi-arid land with an extraordinary history and fantastic sites, like the Roman theater in Mérida. But it also has astonishing valleys like the Valle del Jerte where, every spring, thousands of cherry trees blossom.

Extremadura is also famous for a special aroma. Not far from the Valle del Jerte is the place where they make Pimentón de la Vera: some of the best paprika in the world. Its deep red color is distinctive, but what really makes it notable is its smokiness. Every October, the fields around La Vera valley are full of the smells coming from small smokehouses, where oak fires smolder just below grids holding the region's harvest of red peppers. They become the smoky, sweet paprika that gives its distinctive flavor to many Spanish dishes, especially our cured meats, like chorizo.

The region is also home to extraordinary cheeses—Torta de la Serena from Castuera in Badajoz, Torta del Casar from Casar de Cáceres. These two towns, close to the border with Portugal, produce similar cheeses that capture the almost enchanted spirit of the region. First the milk is curdled with wild cardoon flowers, an unusual method uniquely connected to the land. Then the cheese hardens before changing again, a few weeks later, when it magically liquefies at its core. On the outside, the cheese looks unexceptional, but inside is a completely liquid center. To open the cheese, you make a hole in the top and scoop out the liquid with a wooden spoon. On a recent trip to Extremadura with my family, my girls ate a torta sandwich that a local deli had made for us with some good Ibérico ham, also from Extremadura. Believe me, it's a strong cheese with a big taste for children, but they devoured the sandwiches. My daughters wanted to know why those sandwiches aren't served in the best restaurants in America. The cheeses are fragile and hard to transport, but are available online and in specialty stores. They deserve to be part of the best menus in the world.

Rice may have come to Europe thanks to Alexander the Great, who brought the cereal grass from Persia to the Mediterranean. But it was the Moors who found the best European home for rice, planting the crop in Spain around one thousand years ago. Today, the rice fields close to Valencia produce extraordinary grains that are the basis for Spain's great rice dishes: paellas and arroces. The key to their greatness lies in the special Spanish rice varieties, Bomba and Calasparra, which soak up lots of liquid, doubling in size without turning mushy and losing shape. Paella, named after the round pan in which the rice cooks, may well be the most famous Spanish dish in the world, but if you're used to restaurants serving "paella" made with regular rice, get ready for a revelation. Real Spanish paella relies on the very best rice, mixed with great stock and fresh ingredients. In Valencia, they cook huge paellas outdoors—a tradition that inspired me to do the same in Washington, D.C. Every week there's a farmer's market outside my restaurant in the nation's capital, and I often celebrate the event with a giant paella next to the market stalls. You'd be amazed how quickly Washingtonians can clean up a huge Spanish dish in the middle of the street.

rice

valencia

The Valencia region in eastern Spain will always remind me of my uncle José Luís Catiriela, who played a larger-than-life role in my childhood. He was the uncle who always wrote me special letters when I was doing my military service, offering me wise words of advice as I traveled around the world. When the opportunity came to move to the United States, he was the one who encouraged me to take my chances in the New World, no matter how great the obstacles. He thought there was no better country than the United States, not least because he worked as a doctor at the U.S. military base in Zaragoza and later at the Ford plant outside Valencia. I vividly remember one of my childhood trips to Valencia, during which he took me under his wing and introduced me to a few restaurants. We ate paellas that were simply the best rice dishes in the world, and we devoured local delicacies such as *allipebre,* a simple eel dish from Albufeira prepared with pimentón and oil.

In addition to its rice, Valencia is famous around the world for its citrus. Farmers in other countries have tried to grow clementines as they do near Valencia, but they cannot match the sweetness and delicacy of the Spanish version. Sweetness is a constant here; just one sip of the great dessert wine Moscatel tells you how rich and sunny this region is. Or you could take one bite of the delicious turrón, a nougat made from the region's wonderful almonds and honey, which is a traditional gift at Christmas. You can almost taste the happiness of life in Valencia.

RICE • REIS • RIZ

Arroz con setas, alcachofas y sepia

Rice with mushrooms, artichokes, and cuttlefish

SERVES 4

- 2 MEDIUM ARTICHOKES
- 1 BUNCH FRESH PARSLEY
- ⅓ CUP SPANISH EXTRA-VIRGIN OLIVE OIL
- 10 OUNCES FRESH CUTTLEFISH, CUT INTO SMALL PIECES
- 4 OUNCES FRESH WILD MUSHROOMS, SUCH AS CHANTERELLES
- ½ TEASPOON SAFFRON
- ⅓ CUP SOFRITO (PAGE 247)
- 2 TEASPOONS MINCED GARLIC
- SEA SALT TO TASTE
- 5½ CUPS FLAT MINERAL OR FILTERED WATER
- 1 CUP SPANISH BOMBA OR CALASPARRA RICE
- 1 TEASPOON CHOPPED FRESH PARSLEY

José's Tip:
It's important to use fresh or fresh-frozen cuttlefish (sepia), not the canned product. There is a huge difference in flavor and texture. Traditionally, this dish is served with Allioli (page 250). If you can't find Spanish rice, use another short-grain rice.

Use a serrated knife to cut off the top half of each artichoke. Break off and discard all of the exterior leaves until you reach the pale green, tender center leaves. Pry open the leaves with your fingers and use a spoon to scrape out the white, hairy interior (choke). Use a small knife to peel away the tough outer layer around the base of the artichoke and stem, until you reach the soft white flesh. Don't be afraid to remove most of the artichoke. Cut the trimmed artichoke into 4 quarters and put them into a large bowl of cold water. Add the parsley to stop the artichoke from oxidizing and coloring. Trim and quarter the remaining artichoke and add it to the parsley water.

Heat the olive oil in a large pot over medium-high heat until hot and just smoking. Add the cuttlefish and cook for 2 minutes. Add the mushrooms and cook for 2 more minutes, then add the artichokes and cook for another 2 minutes. Add the saffron, sofrito, and garlic and cook, stirring, for 1 more minute. Season to taste with salt.

Add the mineral water and increase the heat to high. Once the mixture comes to a boil, stir in the rice and cook for 5 minutes. Reduce the heat to low and let the rice simmer for 10 more minutes. (Do not stir the rice again. This could cause the rice to cook unevenly.) The rice will be a little soupy but cooked through. Season to taste with salt and garnish with parsley.

When we talk about *arroz*, we're not just talking about the rice. The plural word *arroces* has the deeper meaning of "rice dishes." You might be wondering where paella fits in. Paella is a rice dish made in a traditional round paella pan. Arroces can be made in any pan and are served on a plate or in a casserole. They can be soupy, while a paella tends to be drier. This dish is somewhere in between.

Paella de bogavante y setas a banda

Lobster and mushroom paella

SERVES 4

FOR THE STOCK

1 RIPE TOMATO, HALVED

½ HEAD GARLIC, PAPERY SKIN REMOVED, HALVED

4 FRESH FLAT-LEAF PARSLEY SPRIGS

1 BAY LEAF

1 1½-POUND LOBSTER

3 BLUE CRABS, FRESH OR FROZEN

3 TABLESPOONS SALMORRA (PAGE 248)

FOR THE RICE

¼ CUP SPANISH EXTRA-VIRGIN OLIVE OIL

8 OUNCES FRESH SEASONAL MUSHROOMS SUCH AS CHANTERELLES, PIOPPINI, AND BEECH

1 CUP SPANISH BOMBA RICE

PINCH OF SAFFRON

SEA SALT TO TASTE

ALLIOLI (PAGE 250)

José's Tip:
If you don't have a paella pan, use a large sauté pan instead. If you can't find Spanish rice, use another short-grain rice.

Prepare the stock: Combine the tomato, garlic, parsley, and bay leaf in a large stockpot. Using a sharp knife, separate the lobster head from the claws and body. Split the lobster head in half and add to the pot. Refrigerate the body and claws until ready to use in the paella. With the same sharp knife, cut the crabs into quarters and add them to the pot. Cover with 2 quarts of water and stir in the salmorra. Bring to a boil over high heat, then reduce the heat to medium-low and simmer the stock for 1 hour.

Remove the stock from the heat. Transfer the lobster head and the crabs, and 2 cups of the stock to a blender and crush the shellfish. Then stir the crushed shellfish mixture back into the pot until well combined. Strain the stock through a fine-mesh strainer or a cheesecloth-lined colander. Press down on the solids with the back of a spoon to release all the liquids. Discard the solids and set the stock aside.

Prepare the rice: Using a sharp knife, cut up the reserved lobster. Separate the claws from the knuckles and slice the tail into 4 pieces. Crack the claws with the knife so they will be easy to pull apart once they are cooked. Cut the knuckles into two pieces.

In a 13-inch paella pan, heat 2 tablespoons of the olive oil over medium heat for 2 minutes until just smoking. Add the lobster pieces and sauté about 1 minute on each side. Transfer the lobster to a plate. Pour 2 more tablespoons of the olive oil into the paella pan, then add the mushrooms and sauté for 2 minutes. Stir in the rice and cook for 1 minute. Pour in 3 cups of the strained stock and stir until well combined, about 30 seconds. Increase the heat to high and cook for 6 minutes. Do not stir the rice again as it may cause the rice to cook unevenly.

Add the saffron and season to taste with salt. Reduce the heat to low and simmer for 11 minutes. After about 6 minutes, add the lobster pieces to the paella to continue to cook for the final 5 minutes. The rice should have absorbed all of the liquid. Remove the paella from the heat, cover with a clean kitchen towel, and let the paella rest for 5 minutes before serving. Serve with spoonfuls of allioli.

The lobsters in America are great, but they are different from the ones we find in Spain. There they live in the wild, and the fishing is heavily regulated. Eating one of those lobsters that has just come out of the sea, with its briny flavor, is a magical experience.

Arroz con conejo y azafrán

Rabbit with saffron rice

SERVES 4 TO 6

3 RIPE PLUM TOMATOES

¼ CUP SPANISH EXTRA-VIRGIN OLIVE OIL, PLUS 2 TABLESPOONS

1 3-POUND RABBIT, CUT INTO 12 PIECES

1 MEDIUM SPANISH ONION, FINELY CHOPPED

1 GREEN BELL PEPPER, SEEDED AND FINELY CHOPPED

5 GARLIC CLOVES, MINCED

1 BAY LEAF

½ TEASPOON SWEET PIMENTÓN (SPANISH SMOKED PAPRIKA)

5 OUNCES SAFFRON MILK CAP MUSHROOMS OR OTHER FRESH WILD MUSHROOMS, SUCH AS CHANTERELLE OR OYSTER

4 CUPS FLAT MINERAL OR FILTERED WATER

1 CUP SPANISH BOMBA OR CALASPARRA RICE

2 PINCHES SAFFRON

4 FRESH THYME SPRIGS

José's Tip:
Serve this dish immediately. If it rests too long, the rice will absorb all the liquid and become soggy. If you can't find Spanish rice, use another short-grain rice.

Slice the tomatoes in half. Place a grater over a mixing bowl. Rub the cut surface of the tomatoes over the grater until all of the flesh is grated. Discard the skins and set the tomato purée aside.

Heat ¼ cup of the olive oil in a large sauté pan over medium heat. Add the rabbit pieces and cook, turning frequently, until the rabbit has browned on all sides, about 15 minutes. Remove the meat to a plate. Reduce the heat to medium-low and add the remaining 2 tablespoons of olive oil to the pan. Add the onion and pepper and cook slowly, stirring often, for 10 minutes. Add the garlic, bay leaf, and pimentón and mix well. Add the reserved tomato purée and cook down for 5 more minutes or until the tomato becomes deep brown in color. Add the mushrooms and increase the heat to medium-high. Cook, stirring, for 3 minutes, until the mushrooms are well combined. Add the rabbit to the pot, along with the juices that have collected on the plate, folding it into the mixture.

Pour in the mineral water, increase the heat to high, and bring to a boil. Stir in the rice and cook for 5 minutes, turning the rabbit pieces while the rice cooks. Reduce the heat to low, add the saffron, and simmer for 10 minutes more without stirring the rice again, which could cause it to cook unevenly. The rice will be a little soupy but cooked through. Remove the pan from the heat. Divide the rice and rabbit among shallow bowls and garnish with the thyme sprigs.

Rabbits have long been a source of protein for the working people in Spain. The pinkish white meat mixes well with Spain's great rice, especially when the meat is cooked until it is ready to fall off the bone and the rice has absorbed the flavor of the meat. This is a satisfying but very delicate dish.

Paella de verduras

Vegetable paella

SERVES 4 TO 6

¼ CUP SPANISH EXTRA-VIRGIN OLIVE OIL

8 BABY YELLOW SQUASH, HALVED LENGTHWISE

1 CUP ½-INCH EGGPLANT CUBES (ABOUT ½ GLOBE EGGPLANT)

3 CUPS CAULIFLOWER FLORETS

¼ POUND FRESH WILD MUSHROOMS, SUCH AS CHANTERELLE OR OYSTER, SLICED

1 TEASPOON MINCED GARLIC

2 RIPE PLUM TOMATOES, DICED

¼ CUP SOFRITO (PAGE 247)

1 CUP DRY WHITE WINE

PINCH OF SAFFRON

3 CUPS FLAT MINERAL OR FILTERED WATER

1 CUP SPANISH BOMBA OR CALASPARRA RICE

2 OUNCES FRESH OR FROZEN GREEN PEAS

SEA SALT TO TASTE

2 OUNCES PIQUILLO PEPPERS, CUT INTO ½-INCH-THICK STRIPS

ALLIOLI (PAGE 250)

Heat the olive oil in a 13-inch paella pan over medium-high heat. Add the squash and brown on each side, about 2 minutes per side. Add the eggplant and cauliflower and cook for 2 minutes, then add the mushrooms and garlic and cook for 2 more minutes. Stir in the plum tomatoes and the sofrito and cook for 1 minute. Pour in the white wine and let it reduce by half, about 2 minutes.

Crumble the saffron into the pan and pour in the mineral water. Increase the heat to high and bring to a boil. Let the mixture boil for 2 to 3 minutes, then add the rice and peas and stir until well combined. Reduce the heat to medium-high, season to taste with salt, and cook for 4 minutes. Do not stir the rice again, as this can cause it to cook unevenly.

After 4 minutes, reduce the heat to low, lay the pepper strips on top of the paella, and cook for another 7 minutes. Remove the paella from the heat, cover with a clean kitchen towel, and let rest for 5 minutes before serving. Serve with spoonfuls of allioli.

José's Tip:
It's best to use vegetables that are in season. Always start with the vegetables that take the longest to cook, then move them to the periphery of the paella pan as you add more vegetables. If you don't have a paella pan, use a large sauté pan instead. If you can't find Spanish rice, use another short-grain rice.

Over the years, my American friends have told me about the difficulty of finding vegetables on the menus in Spanish restaurants. When you visit Spanish markets, you see vegetables everywhere, so what is going on? Many of our regions produce astonishing vegetables, like cauliflower and white asparagus, and there are even restaurants that specialize in those vegetables when they are at the peak of their season. The truth is that Spaniards love vegetables, and this vegetable paella suggests my friends are looking at the wrong parts of the menus.

Walk into the market in any Spanish town or city and you'll usually notice a crowd around a single counter: the best fish-seller. To outsiders, there may be no discernible difference between the meticulous arrangement of fish, piled high on a bed of glistening ice, at the best fish stall and the similar display at the next stall. But to locals, the freshness and quality of their respective offerings will be worlds apart. That's how picky the Spanish are when it comes to fish. The result is that you can walk into small supermarkets across the country and buy fresh, flavorful fish in a way you, sadly, can't in most bigger stores across the United States.

Spanish cooks use many different techniques to savor the taste of the sea. In the south, they are experts at frying fish; in the Basque country and Catalonia, wonderful fishermen's stews are served all over. In every region, cooks use simple, careful methods to preserve the delicate flavors and textures of fish, like grilling over charcoal or baking in a thick casing of salt.

The downside to this pursuit of quality is overfishing. The Spanish fishing fleet is second only to the Japanese in size, and both countries value the extraordinary treasures that swim in Spanish waters, including the magnificent Mediterranean tuna caught in the almadraba off the coast of Andalusia. But each year, they catch fewer and fewer of the great fish that have swum into these intricate nets since Moorish times. The traditional fishing fleets are not the problem. Modern technology has allowed unscrupulous fishermen to track ever smaller fish in remoter parts of the oceans. If we're not careful, our children will never see the kind of overflowing market stalls that are so inspiring in Spain.

fish

VENTA
DE ARRO
CALASPAR

murcia

My wife and I like to drive through Spain, even though flying often makes more sense. We love watching the countryside roll by and stopping in the little towns and villages along the way. After living in the United States for so many years, this feels like the only way to reacquaint ourselves with Spain. Every time we go there, we feel a deep sense of rediscovery—as if we're looking through a new lens at something strangely familiar.

On one of our many trips we drove through Murcia, in Spain's Mediterranean south. We stopped in the town of Lorca, where I found a great restaurant popular with truck drivers. Its customers were varied and so was its menu; there was something for everyone. There were inexpensive sandwiches for snacks, and hearty stews if you needed something more substantial. It also served some of the best seafood from the Mediterranean—at prices that seemed exorbitant for a roadside stop.

The section of the menu that caught my attention, though, was a selection of trigo, something I had heard of and read about but never eaten. *Trigo* is a generic name for wheat and wheat dishes, and the restaurant offered several varieties of wheat stews. This isn't a dish you can cook at the last minute. The wheat is prepared the day before, to soften it up. The next morning, the restaurant made the softened wheat into several versions of stews in huge casseroles, serving them until there was nothing left. The one I recall (because I devoured it) was trigo de conejo—a rabbit stew.

Murcia has other great food and drink, of course. There's the amazing fish and seafood of its coastline. There is the extraordinary Calasparra rice, which is so good at absorbing sauces and stocks. There are the incredible fruits and vegetables, including the biggest lemon groves you've ever seen. Murcia has its drunken goat cheese (a goat's cheese that soaks in wine for 72 hours before curing) and its great Jumilla wine, made from the Monastrell grape.

Lubina a la sal

Salt-baked red snapper

SERVES 4

3 POUNDS SEA SALT OR KOSHER SALT

4 BAY LEAVES

6 FRESH ROSEMARY SPRIGS

10 FRESH THYME SPRIGS

1 WHOLE SNAPPER, APPROXIMATELY 2½ POUNDS, GUTTED BUT NOT SCALED

2 TABLESPOONS SPANISH EXTRA-VIRGIN OLIVE OIL

Preheat the oven to 375°F.

In a large bowl, mix the salt with 3 tablespoons water, stirring until the salt is slightly damp. Add 2 bay leaves, 3 rosemary sprigs, and 5 thyme sprigs and mix well. Spread half of the salt mixture on a baking sheet and lay the remaining herbs on top. Place the red snapper on top of the herbs and cover the fish completely with the remaining salt mixture, making sure to pack it firmly around the fish.

Bake the fish for 30 minutes on the middle rack of your oven, then let it rest for 5 minutes. Using a fork and spoon, crack open the side of the salt crust. The upper half of the salt, now a hard shell, should lift off easily.

With the help of a fork, gently peel away the skin and discard. Using a knife, cut below the head through to the bone. Then cut along the spine and carefully lift the meat off the bone and set aside. Turn the fish over and repeat on the other side. Season the fish with salt and olive oil and serve.

There's no better or simpler technique for cooking fish than this. The fish encased inside the salt shell is soft and moist, with no hint of saltiness, in spite of what you might expect. You normally see this dish in restaurants, but it's easy to replicate at home.

José's Tip:
Temperature, cooking time, and the weight of the fish need to be precise. I recommend placing a thermometer in your oven to make sure your temperature is correct. After you make this dish a few times, you'll discover the right combination to give you a perfectly cooked fish.

Ventresca de atún con semillas de sésamo y pimientos del piquillo

Seared tuna belly with sesame seeds and piquillo pepper

SERVES 4

1 7.6-OUNCE JAR OF PIQUILLO PEPPERS (ABOUT 12 PEPPERS)

5 TABLESPOONS SPANISH EXTRA-VIRGIN OLIVE OIL

SEA SALT TO TASTE

4 6-OUNCE PIECES OF TORO (BEST-QUALITY TUNA BELLY)

2 CUPS SESAME SEEDS

CHERVIL LEAVES (OPTIONAL)

In a blender, purée half the piquillo peppers from the jar along with 1/2 cup of their juice. Transfer the pepper purée to a mixing bowl, stir in 3 tablespoons of the olive oil, and season to taste with salt.

Season the tuna pieces on both sides with salt. Spread the sesame seeds on a plate and roll the tuna pieces in the sesame seeds. Heat the remaining 2 tablespoons olive oil in a medium sauté pan over medium heat until hot and just beginning to smoke. Place the tuna pieces in the pan and cook for 2 minutes on each side, until the sesame seeds are browned. Transfer the tuna pieces to a plate and keep warm.

Add the remaining peppers to the sauté pan and sear, about 2 minutes per side. To serve, divide the seared peppers among 4 plates. Cut each piece of tuna into 3 slices and lay on top of the peppers. Drizzle with the pepper purée and garnish with chervil, if you like.

José's Tip:
You can use tuna loin here if you have trouble finding good-quality tuna belly.

Spanish cooks have used sesame seeds, especially in desserts, since Muslims arrived in Spain. Here they add a nice flavor to the tuna, and they protect the fish from the heat. When the seeds are warmed, they release a rich aroma. It's a great way to cook any fish, especially tuna.

"Pixin" al estilo de Tazones

Monkfish, Tazones style

SERVES 4

4 CUPS SPANISH EXTRA-VIRGIN OLIVE OIL

4 6-OUNCE MONKFISH FILLETS

1 LEMON, HALVED

3 LARGE EGGS

2 CUPS ALL-PURPOSE FLOUR

SEA SALT TO TASTE

Heat the olive oil in a deep pot over medium-high heat until it measures 325°F on a candy thermometer.

Cut each monkfish fillet into 4 medallions and squeeze the juice from the lemon halves over the medallions. Whisk the eggs in a small bowl and pour the flour into another bowl. Working in batches, dredge the medallions in the flour, then dip in the egg. Gently drop 4 to 6 medallions into the hot oil at a time.

Using tongs, carefully turn the monkfish pieces over in the hot oil so they brown evenly. Cook for 2 to 3 minutes, then transfer to a paper towel-lined plate to drain. Allow the oil to return to 325°F between batches. Season to taste with salt and serve immediately.

In Tazones, on the northern coast of Spain, you can see monkfish hung to dry briefly in the sun and the sea breeze. It is an extraordinary sight; the first time you go there, you have to rub your eyes to make sure you're not dreaming. They cook the monkfish by dipping it in a simple batter and frying it—one of my favorite ways to eat this meaty fish.

Bacalao al pil pil

Salt cod with garlic and olive oil

SERVES 4

4 4-OUNCE TOP-QUALITY SALT COD FILLETS (SEE TIP)

4 GARLIC CLOVES, PEELED

¼ CUP SPANISH EXTRA-VIRGIN OLIVE OIL

2 BAY LEAVES

1 GUINDILLA CHILE PEPPER (OR YOUR FAVORITE DRIED CHILE PEPPER), CRACKED AND SEEDED

Put the cod in a large bowl, skin side up. Cover with water, and refrigerate for 36 hours, changing the water at least 3 times to remove the salt. When changing the water, however, reserve about one-third of the soaking liquid so the fish will retain some of the salty flavor. (The soaking time needed to release the salt from the fish may vary depending on the thickness of your salt cod.) Drain the cod and pat dry with a paper towel.

Split open the garlic cloves by pressing down with the heel of your hand or with the flat side of a kitchen knife. Heat the olive oil in a medium nonstick sauté pan over medium-low heat. Add the garlic and cook until golden, about 2 minutes. Remove the garlic and set aside.

Reduce the heat under the pan to low. Add the bay leaves, chile pepper, and the cod, skin side down, and cook for 8 to 10 minutes. Turn the cod over and cook for another 8 to 10 minutes until cooked through. Carefully transfer the cod to a plate, flesh side down, and keep warm. Remove the bay leaves and chile pepper and set aside.

Once you eat bacalao al pil pil, with its subtle flavor and sauce, you wonder how it was created. The mixture of garlic and olive oil creates an emulsion with the gelatins of the fish, and the result is quite magical. This technique might seem new, but it's been used in Spain for centuries.

Remove the pan from the heat and gently shake it in a circular motion. You will see the white balls of natural gelatin that were released from the cod. This gelatin will cause the sauce to emulsify. Using the bottom of a small fine-mesh strainer, gently whisk the oil and gelatin together, while you shake the pan, until it emulsifies into a thick creamy liquid, 10 to 15 minutes. (Do not get frustrated if your sauce takes longer to emulsify; it may take up to 30 minutes.)

Return the cod to the pan and heat over low heat to warm through. (Be careful not to overheat the sauce and cause it to break apart.) To serve, spoon some sauce onto each plate. Place a cod fillet on top, skin side up, and garnish with the reserved garlic pieces, bay leaves, and chile pepper.

José's Tip:
It is important to use the best-quality salt cod you can find. Look for brands like Giraldo from the Basque region of Spain. These cod fillets are also available with the salt removed, so you can skip the soaking at the start of this recipe. To test if your cod needs to keep soaking, pinch off a bit of fish from the center of the piece and taste.

Marmitako

Traditional Basque stew of tuna, potatoes, pepper, and onions

This dish got its start over a tiny burner on a fishing boat. It features the beautiful bonito tuna, caught in the north of Spain, plus one or two ingredients that could survive a sailing trip. As they say in the Basque country, no marmitako is better than the one your mother makes at home, so if you are there, go to a bar, make a new friend, and ask him to take you home to eat his mother's tuna stew.

SERVES 4 TO 6

- 1 POUND FRESH BONITO OR YELLOWFIN TUNA
- 2 MEDIUM GREEN BELL PEPPERS
- ½ CUP SPANISH EXTRA-VIRGIN OLIVE OIL, PLUS MORE FOR DRIZZLING
- 2 SLICES DAY-OLD BREAD
- 1 POUND RIPE PLUM TOMATOES
- 3 CUPS THINLY SLICED ONIONS
- 2 TABLESPOONS MINCED GARLIC
- 1 POUND RUSSET POTATOES, PEELED AND CHOPPED
- ½ CUP DRY WHITE WINE
- ¼ CUP BRANDY
- 1 GUINDILLA CHILE PEPPER (OR YOUR FAVORITE DRIED CHILE PEPPER)
- 2 TEASPOONS SWEET PIMENTÓN (SPANISH SMOKED PAPRIKA)
- SEA SALT TO TASTE
- 1 TABLESPOON CHOPPED FRESH PARSLEY LEAVES

José's Tip:
If you break the potatoes into chunks rather than chopping them, the potatoes release more of their starch into the sauce. Hold the potato in your hand and using a small knife, dig into the potato and lift off a chunk. You will see the potato fibers pull apart, allowing the starch to escape more easily while cooking.

Preheat the broiler.

Cut the tuna into 1-inch cubes. Put the cubes on a plate, cover with plastic wrap, and refrigerate.

Roast the bell peppers under the broiler, turning them as they brown. Transfer the peppers to a bowl, cover with plastic wrap, and steam for 10 minutes. When cool enough to handle, peel the peppers, discard the skin, and remove the seeds. Slice the peppers into 2-inch strips and set aside.

In a small saucepan, heat ¼ cup of the olive oil over medium heat. Fry the bread until golden, 2 to 3 minutes on each side. Transfer to a paper towel–lined plate to drain.

Slice the tomatoes in half. Place a grater over a mixing bowl. Rub the cut surface of the tomatoes over the grater until all of the flesh is grated. Discard the skins.

In a 12-quart stockpot, heat the remaining ¼ cup of olive oil over medium-low heat. Add the onions, garlic, and roasted peppers and cook until golden brown, about 20 minutes. Add the potatoes and cook for 3 minutes, then add the wine and brandy and cook until the alcohol evaporates. Stir in the tomato pulp, guindilla pepper, and pimentón and cook for another 10 minutes. Fold in the fried bread and continue to cook for 2 more minutes. Pour in 3 cups of water, cover, and cook for 15 minutes. Shake the pot gently while it cooks to prevent the potatoes from sticking to the bottom of the pot.

Season the chilled tuna with salt and stir into the pot. Cover and cook for 3 minutes. The tuna should be juicy inside and barely cooked through. Remove the pot from the heat and season to taste with salt. Garnish each serving with chopped parsley and a drizzle of olive oil.

Suquet de escórpora con almejas

Scorpion fish stew with clams

SERVES 4

FOR THE STOCK

1 GARLIC CLOVE, PEELED

1 TABLESPOON SPANISH EXTRA-VIRGIN OLIVE OIL

½ CELERY STALK, ROUGHLY CHOPPED

½ CARROT, TRIMMED AND ROUGHLY CHOPPED

½ MEDIUM SPANISH ONION, PEELED AND ROUGHLY CHOPPED

1 3-POUND SCORPION FISH, FILLETED, HEAD AND BONES RESERVED (SEE TIP)

FOR THE SUQUET

2 RIPE PLUM TOMATOES

2 TABLESPOONS SPANISH EXTRA-VIRGIN OLIVE OIL

2 RUSSET POTATOES, PEELED AND ROUGHLY CHOPPED

PINCH OF SUGAR

PINCH OF SAFFRON

¼ TEASPOON SWEET PIMENTÓN (SPANISH SMOKED PAPRIKA)

FOR THE PICADA

2 GARLIC CLOVES, PEELED

PINCH OF SEA SALT

2 TABLESPOONS CHOPPED FRESH FLAT-LEAF PARSLEY

SEA SALT TO TASTE

8 MANILLA CLAMS, SCRUBBED

ALLIOLI (PAGE 250; OPTIONAL)

Prepare the stock: Split the garlic clove by pressing down hard on it with the heel of your hand or the flat side of a kitchen knife. In a large pot, heat the olive oil over medium-low heat. Add the garlic, celery, carrot, and onion and sauté until golden brown, about 10 minutes. Add the fish bones and head and enough water to cover. Bring to a simmer, then reduce the heat and simmer gently for 25 minutes. Skim any foam that rises to the top.

Prepare the suquet: Slice the tomatoes in half. Place a grater over a mixing bowl. Rub the cut surface of the tomatoes over the grater until all of the flesh is grated. Discard the skins. In a deep pot, heat the olive oil over medium heat. Add the potatoes and sauté for 2 minutes. Stir in the tomato pulp and sugar and cook for another 2 minutes, then add the saffron and pimentón and cook for a minute.

Strain the fish stock through a fine-mesh strainer, then add just enough stock to the pot to cover the potatoes. Increase the heat to medium-high and bring to a boil, then reduce the heat to low and simmer until the potatoes are cooked through, about 10 minutes.

Prepare the picada: Using a mortar and pestle, mash the garlic with the salt until you have a thick paste. Add the parsley and one piece of potato from the stew and mix.

Salt the fish fillets on both sides and cut in half, so you have 4 equal pieces. Place the fillets in the pot and add the clams. Cook for 4 to 5 minutes or until the clams begin to open. Stir in the picada and season to taste with salt. Serve with allioli, if you like.

José's Tip:
The spiny scorpion fish has tasty white flesh and can be bought by special order in the United States. This stew can also be made with any firm-fleshed fish, such as monkfish or red snapper.

When you've been cooking since the age of fourteen, you find that many of your friends are chefs. Quim Marqués is one of my best friends, and he actually comes from a family of chefs. If you're in Barcelona, make sure you go to his restaurant, El Suquet de L'Amirall. Tell them you're my friend, and you'll see how good the food is when people cook for friends. This is one of Quim's great fish stews. Try it with your own family and friends.

Sancocho

Fish and potato stew

SERVES 4

FOR THE MOJO SAUCE

3 GARLIC CLOVES

1 SMALL GUINDILLA CHILE PEPPER OR OTHER DRIED HOT PEPPER

½ TEASPOON SWEET PIMENTÓN (SPANISH SMOKED PAPRIKA)

½ TEASPOON SEA SALT

1 TEASPOON SPANISH EXTRA-VIRGIN OLIVE OIL

FOR THE STEW

1 BAY LEAF

1 SMALL SPANISH ONION, PEELED AND QUARTERED

1 SMALL RED BELL PEPPER, SEEDED AND CUT INTO 2-INCH STRIPS

6 SPRIGS FRESH FLAT-LEAF PARSLEY

1 POUND YUKON GOLD POTATOES, PEELED AND CHOPPED

1 POUND SWEET POTATOES, PEELED AND CHOPPED

SEA SALT TO TASTE

4 6-OUNCE SEA BASS FILLETS

Prepare the sauce: Using a mortar and pestle, mash the garlic, guindilla pepper, pimentón, and salt into a paste. Keep turning the mortar clockwise while mashing and scrape down the paste from the sides of the mortar with the pestle. Slowly pour in the olive oil and continue mashing until the oil is well incorporated, then set the sauce aside.

Prepare the stew: Put the bay leaf, onion, bell pepper, parsley, potatoes, and sweet potatoes into a medium saucepan, add 4 cups of water, and bring to a boil over high heat. Reduce the heat to medium-low and cook until tender, about 20 minutes. Stir 1 teaspoon of the cooking liquid into the sauce in the mortar. Season to taste with more salt, then stir the sauce into the pan.

Season the sea bass with salt and add the fillets to the pan. Cook for 6 to 7 minutes or until the fillets are cooked through. Transfer the fillets to serving bowls and ladle several ounces of broth over each. Place some potatoes, sweet potatoes, onions, parsley, and red pepper around the fillets and top the fillets with a spoonful of the mojo sauce.

I first ate sancocho on my first trip to the Canary Islands, so imagine my surprise when I was in New York a year later and saw the same word on the menu of a Latin American restaurant. It had some of the same characteristics, underscoring the importance of the Canary Islands as a stepping stone between Europe and Latin America.

José's Tip:
Don't let the liquid come to a boil once the fish is added. The stew should cook low and slow so the fish doesn't break apart in the broth.

Buñuelos de Bacalao

Cod fritters

SERVES 4

1¼ POUNDS SALT COD

1¼ POUNDS RUSSET POTATOES, PEELED AND BOILED

4½ CUPS SPANISH EXTRA-VIRGIN OLIVE OIL

1 TEASPOON MINCED GARLIC

1 CUP ALL-PURPOSE FLOUR

5 LARGE EGGS

1 TEASPOON CHOPPED FLAT-LEAF PARSLEY

¼ TEASPOON GROUND WHITE PEPPER

SEA SALT TO TASTE

2 EGG WHITES

José's Tip:
It is important to use the best-quality salt cod you can find. Look for brands like Giraldo from the Basque region of Spain. These cod fillets are also available with the salt removed, so you can skip the soaking at the start of this recipe. To test if your cod needs to keep soaking, pinch off a bit of fish from the center of the piece and taste.

Put the cod in a large bowl, skin side up. Cover with water and refrigerate for 36 hours, changing the water at least 3 times to remove the salt. Each time you change the water, reserve about one-third of the previous batch of soaking liquid so the fish retains some of the salty flavor. (The soaking time needed to release the salt from the fish varies depending on the thickness of your salt cod.) Drain the cod and pat dry with a paper towel.

In a medium sauté pan, bring ½ cup water to a simmer over medium-high heat. Add the cod and cook until tender and easy to break apart with the back of a wooden spoon, about 8 minutes. Using a slotted spoon, transfer the cod to a plate and cool. Reserve the cod cooking water. When the cod is cool enough to handle, shred it with your fingers and set aside.

Purée the potatoes with a potato masher or in a standing kitchen mixer fitted with the paddle attachment and set aside. Pour the reserved cod cooking water and ½ cup of the olive oil into a medium pot, add the garlic, and heat over medium-low heat for 1 minute. Add the flour and puréed potatoes and mix well with a wooden spoon. Remove the pot from the heat and stir in the eggs, 1 at a time. Then fold in the parsley and shredded cod until well combined. Add the pepper and salt to taste. Lightly whisk the egg whites into a light foam in a separate bowl and fold them into the cod-potato mixture. Refrigerate the mixture, covered, for 2 hours or overnight.

Buñuelos is a term that usually applies to dough that is deep-fried—yet another sign of Spain's world-beating position as a producer of olive oil. In Spain, we'll deep-fry anything in olive oil, including desserts that are fried and sprinkled with cinnamon and sugar. This is a savory version of fritters made with salt cod. Don't assume the worst about the preserved nature of the fish. A good salt cod is more expensive, and generally of better quality, than most fresh cod.

Heat the remaining 4 cups olive oil in a pot to 325°F (measured on a candy thermometer). Working in batches, carefully drop tablespoon-size scoops of the mixture into the hot oil and fry until golden, 3 to 4 minutes, turning often. Transfer the fritters to a paper towel–lined plate to drain. (The fritters should remain a little moist inside; overcooked fritters will be very dry.) Allow the oil to return to 325°F between batches. Season with salt and serve warm.

Sardinas a la parrilla

Grilled sardines

SERVES 4

8 FRESH SARDINES, SCALED AND GUTTED

SPANISH EXTRA-VIRGIN OLIVE OIL

SEA SALT TO TASTE

Brush the sardines lightly with olive oil and season with salt. Lay the sardines on a grill over hot charcoals or a high flame and cook for 1 to 2 minutes on each side. Transfer to a platter and garnish with more salt and a drizzle of olive oil. If you want to fillet the sardines before serving, hold the sardine with its belly flat on the platter. With your other hand, pinch the tail and pull up toward the head. The spine and bones should pull out easily, leaving two fillets.

My time in Washington, D.C., has taught me that among those things that unite America and Spain, one stands out: Sunday home cooking over a grill or barbecue. We all need to add more fish to our diet, so move away from the ribs and burgers and try these sardines at your next backyard barbecue. They are simply grilled, with no special preparation. Don't worry about their low price; just be grateful more people haven't discovered how delicious they are. My philosophy is to treat every ingredient as if it cost $1,000 a pound, and these taste as if they should.

Merluza a la sidra

Hake in Spanish cider

SERVES 4

¼ CUP PLUS 1 TABLESPOON SPANISH EXTRA-VIRGIN OLIVE OIL, PLUS MORE FOR DRIZZLING

1 GRANNY SMITH APPLE, CORED, PEELED, AND CUT INTO ½-INCH SLICES

SEA SALT TO TASTE

½ MEDIUM SPANISH ONION, THINLY SLICED

1 FRESH THYME SPRIG

2 CUPS SIDRA (SPANISH HARD CIDER)

4 6-OUNCE HAKE FILLETS, SKIN ON

1 TABLESPOON CHOPPED FRESH PARSLEY

Heat 1 tablespoon of the olive oil in a sauté pan over medium-high heat. Add the apple and a pinch of salt and sauté until the apples are browned, about 4 minutes on each side. Transfer to a paper towel–lined plate and drain.

Pour the remaining ¼ cup olive oil into the same sauté pan and reduce the heat to medium-low. Add the onion and thyme and cook until the onion is soft and translucent, about 10 minutes. Pour in the sidra and cook until the liquid is reduced by three-quarters, about 3 minutes.

Lay the hake, skin side down, in the sauté pan and cook on one side for 2 to 3 minutes. (If the fillets are thick, cook for 4 to 5 minutes.) Gently shake the pan, spooning the sauce over the fish as it cooks. Turn the fish over and continue cooking for another 2 to 3 minutes. Add the apple slices, season to taste with salt, and drizzle with olive oil. Divide the hake and apples among 4 plates, spoon the sauce over the hake, and garnish with parsley.

José's Tip:

Use a good-quality, locally made hard cider if you can't find Spanish sidra. A farm-fresh apple cider will also work nicely if you prefer to avoid alcohol.

Every place seems to have its favorite alcoholic drink. Asturias is too cold and rainy for grapes to thrive there, but apples are plentiful, and sidra, or hard cider, is the favorite drink of the region. It's no surprise that Asturians have used hard cider creatively in their kitchens, as in this wonderful dish with hake.

To understand Spain's devotion to seafood, you need to travel to the rough Galician coastline, on the northwestern tip of Spain. In the stunning fjordlike estuaries of the Rías Baixas are nurseries and beds where the locals farm mussels on wooden rafts. Off the coast, you can find fishermen braving some of the wildest seas in Europe. But even their courage pales next to that of the men who cling to the rocks of the coast of death—La Costa de la Muerte. There you'll find the goose-necked barnacles, or percebes, which are highly prized for their flavor of the sea. The only problem is that they must be hacked off the rocks one by one, often under the crashing force of an Atlantic wave. There was a time, in the last century, when seafood was so plentiful in Galicia that it was treated as food for the poor and barnacles were used as fertilizer in the fields. Today, after many years of overfishing, percebes are the most expensive seafood on the menu in many high-end restaurants in Spain—costing more than $100 a pound at Christmas—which almost makes it worth risking life and limb to catch them.

Take a look at the fish stall in any Spanish market, and you'll see an incredible variety of seafood. We cook with squid and octopus, lobster and crab, shrimp and crayfish, oysters and clams. Much Spanish seafood is not available in the United States. But American seafood can be just as exciting to cook and eat; from the extraordinary softshell crabs of the northeast coast to the delicious oysters of the Pacific, and from the shrimp of the Gulf of Mexico to the great lobsters of Maine. I have spent fifteen years cooking Spanish seafood dishes in America; now it's your turn.

seafood

galicia

I once read that falling in love with a place is like sighting dry land after weeks of sailing at sea. That was literally true for me when I first visited Galicia. I was in the navy, sailing on a beautiful tall ship called the *Juan Sebastían Elcano* that had taken me to America for the first time. After seven months of traveling around the world, the first Spanish land we saw was the Galician coast, and we disembarked at Marín, the home of the Spanish naval academy. Back on solid ground, the first dish I ate was a simple plate of Galician-style octopus—pulpo a la Gallega—made from the octopus that lives off the region's rocky coast. The octopus is dusted with smoky Spanish pimentón (paprika), drizzled with a little olive oil, and sprinkled with sea salt from the same ocean that was once home to the octopus. This is a dish you find on menus across Spain, so when I bit into the thick tentacles, I smiled from ear to ear. I had never been to Galicia before, but as soon as I ate that octopus, I knew I was back home.

Galicia is famous for its traditional food, not just its seafood. There are the creamy cheeses called Tetilla and San Simón, both made from the milk of the Rubia Gallega cow (whose name translates as the Blonde Galician). Classic dishes like tortilla de patatas—Spanish potato omelet—are perfected and rightfully celebrated here.

For many Europeans, Galicia is also a deeply mystical place, thanks to the great cathedral of Santiago de Compostela. In the middle ages, Santiago was the third most important pilgrimage site after Jerusalem and Rome. The body of St. James is said to have arrived here after traveling by boat along the Ulla River and passing through the town of Padrón.

For me, the most fascinating stories about the Santiago pilgrims involve food and drink. I love the great tradition of the queimada, or wine punch, which is set on fire as the locals utter a traditional prayer to ward off bad spirits. Many people travel to Santiago to marvel at the cathedral's relics. But my eye is always drawn to the representation of hell on the great cathedral portico. It's a carving of a sinner suspended upside down over a plate of Galicia's famous empanadas, or turnovers, which lie just out of reach. I can't imagine anything more painful.

I make my own pilgrimage to Padrón—not for the saint, but for little green peppers. Fried quickly in olive oil, with a seasoning of salt, the padrón peppers are deliciously crunchy. Most are sweet, but every now and again you'll find one that is hot, which adds a little thrill to the dish.

Bar
O'Bar
RESTAURANTE
SAN JAIME
43
PIMERBON

Vieiras con Albariño

Taylor Bay scallops with Albariño wine

SERVES 4

2 TABLESPOONS SPANISH EXTRA-VIRGIN OLIVE OIL, PLUS MORE FOR DRIZZLING

1 CUP DICED ONIONS

2 GARLIC CLOVES, MINCED

¼ CUP ALBARIÑO WINE, PLUS 2 TEASPOONS

1 TABLESPOON FINELY CHOPPED JAMÓN SERRANO (SPANISH CURED HAM)

2 TEASPOONS CHOPPED FRESH FLAT-LEAF PARSLEY

SEA SALT TO TASTE

8 TAYLOR BAY SCALLOPS IN THEIR SHELLS

3 TABLESPOONS FRESH BREADCRUMBS

Heat the olive oil in a medium sauté pan over low heat, add the onions, and cook until golden brown, about 30 minutes. Stir in the garlic and cook for another 2 minutes, then add ¼ cup of the wine and simmer until the wine has evaporated and the onions have caramelized to a deep golden brown. Set aside to cool, then stir in the ham and 1 teaspoon of parsley and season to taste with salt.

Preheat the broiler.

Gently pry open the scallop shells by running a paring knife through the scallop muscle to separate it from the shell. Be careful not to break the shells. Remove and discard the dark stomach. Using your finger, pull away and discard the tough adductor muscle, which wraps partially around the scallop. Remove the scallops and set aside. Thoroughly wash and dry the bottom shells. Discard the top shells.

Arrange the scallop shells on a baking sheet. Put 1 teaspoon of the onion-ham mixture in each shell and sprinkle with salt. Divide the scallops among the shells, sprinkle them with the remaining wine, and then cover with breadcrumbs. Drizzle with olive oil and broil until the breadcrumbs are golden brown and the scallops are cooked, about 2 minutes. Sprinkle with the remaining parsley and serve immediately.

José's Tip:
If you can't find Taylor Bay scallops, use sea scallops instead.

Here are two ingredients that come from the same region of Galicia: tiny scallops (like Taylor Bay scallops) and the white wine called Albariño. The briny and sweet scallops complement the acidity and fruitiness of the wine, making a wonderful tapa together.

Ostras con vinagreta de cava

Oysters with cava vinegar dressing

SERVES 4

¼ CUP SMALL CAPERS (OR REGULAR CAPERS, ROUGHLY CHOPPED)

½ CUP MANZANILLA OR SPANISH OLIVES, PITTED AND SLICED INTO STRIPS

4 TABLESPOONS SPANISH EXTRA-VIRGIN OLIVE OIL

1 TEASPOON FINELY CHOPPED SHALLOTS

1 TABLESPOON SPANISH CAVA VINEGAR OR CHAMPAGNE VINEGAR

12 KUSHI OYSTERS OR OTHER SMALL WEST COAST OYSTERS SUCH AS KUMAMOTOS

1 TABLESPOON FINELY CHOPPED CHIVES

Mix the capers, olives, and 1 tablespoon of the olive oil together in a small bowl and set aside.

In another bowl, whisk together the shallots, cava vinegar, and the remaining olive oil. Shuck the oysters and detach the meat from the bottom shell, making sure not to spill any of the oyster juices. Remove the oysters from the bottom shells and transfer to a plate. Set the bottom shells on a serving tray and discard the top shells.

Put 1 teaspoon of the olive-caper mixture into each bottom shell with the oyster juices. Top each with an oyster and spoon the cava vinegar dressing over it. Garnish with chives.

I have really learned to appreciate oysters since I moved to the United States, but one thing I've never loved is the mignonette sauce that always accompanies them. I find the vinegar and shallots just too acidic for the delicate oysters. By using cava vinegar, made from Spanish sparkling wine, we're adding a much more refined acidity to match the oysters'.

José's Tip:
You can drop unshucked oysters in boiling water for 45 seconds to make them a bit easier to open. Don't worry; the oysters will still be raw and juicy.

Mejillones a la Gallega

Steamed mussels with bay leaf, pimentón, and potato

SERVES 4

1 POUND YUKON GOLD POTATOES

SEA SALT TO TASTE

32 MUSSELS

1 BAY LEAF

¼ CUP SPANISH EXTRA-VIRGIN OLIVE OIL

½ TEASPOON SWEET PIMENTÓN (SPANISH SMOKED PAPRIKA)

Boil the potatoes in a pot of salted water until easily pierced with a fork, about 25 minutes.

Meanwhile, put the mussels in a medium pot, with the bay leaf and 1 cup water. Cover the pot and bring to a boil over high heat to steam the mussels. As the mussels open, transfer them to a mixing bowl with tongs or a slotted spoon. Once all the mussels have opened, use a paring knife to separate the mussels from their shells, holding the mussels over the mixing bowl to catch any juices. Set the mussels aside. Strain the juices that have collected in the mixing bowl into a small pot, bring to a boil, and reduce by two-thirds, about 2 minutes. Transfer to a mixing bowl and set aside to cool to room temperature. Whisk the olive oil into the reduced juice and add the mussels. Set aside to marinate for about 5 minutes.

Drain the potatoes and peel as soon as possible so the skins come off easily. Return the potatoes to the pot and mash roughly.

Divide the potatoes among 4 plates and top each with about 8 mussels. Spoon some of the marinade over the potatoes, then sprinkle with pimentón and season to taste with sea salt.

When you see a dish that is cooked "a la Gallega," it means it comes from Galicia—and normally involves octopus. The technique is easy: You boil the octopus, serving it with olive oil and pimentón. If you like the sound of that, you can make anything a la Gallega—like these mussels.

José's Tip:
The mussels can be refrigerated in their marinade for 2 to 3 days. The marinated mussels make a great tapa on their own.

Chipirones con cebolla caramelizada

Baby squid with caramelized onions

SERVES 4

- 1/4 CUP PLUS 1 TABLESPOON SPANISH EXTRA-VIRGIN OLIVE OIL
- 1 GARLIC CLOVE, FINELY CHOPPED
- 1 MEDIUM SPANISH ONION, THINLY SLICED
- 1 MEDIUM GREEN BELL PEPPER, SEEDED AND THINLY SLICED
- 1 BAY LEAF
- 1/4 CUP PLUS 2 TABLESPOONS DRY WHITE WINE
- 8 SMALL WHOLE SQUID, CLEANED, BODIES AND TENTACLES SEPARATED
- SEA SALT TO TASTE
- 1 TEASPOON CHOPPED FRESH PARSLEY

Heat 1/4 cup of the olive oil in a medium sauté pan over low heat. Add three-quarters of the garlic and cook until golden, about 1 minute. Add the onion, pepper, and bay leaf, increase the heat to medium-low, and cook, stirring often, until the onion is golden brown, about 20 minutes. You want the onion to caramelize. If it gets too dark, add 1/2 tablespoon water to keep it from burning while it cooks. Add the wine and continue cooking until the alcohol evaporates, about 5 minutes.

Chop 4 of the squid tentacles, add them to the onion and cook for 2 more minutes. Set the mixture aside to cool. When cool enough to handle, stuff each of the squid tubes with 1 tablespoon of the mixture. Set the remaining mixture aside and keep warm.

Season the stuffed tubes and remaining tentacles with salt. Heat 1 tablespoon of the olive oil in a large sauté pan over medium-high heat. Add the stuffed tubes and tentacles and brown, about 2 minutes on each side. Stir in the remaining garlic and the parsley and remove the pan from the heat.

Divide the remaining onion mixture among 4 plates. Top each with 2 stuffed tubes and 1 tentacle and drizzle with any liquid from the sauté pan.

I love the texture and the sweetness of squid, especially baby ones. Close to my home in Maryland is a Korean fish market that often sells beautiful, sweet fresh squid. And nothing goes better with this squid than a caramelized, marmaladey kind of onion. They make a delicious tapa together.

Tortilla de camarones

Shrimp fritters

SERVES 4

4 CUPS SPANISH EXTRA-VIRGIN OLIVE OIL

½ CUP CHICKPEA (GARBANZO) FLOUR

½ CUP ALL-PURPOSE FLOUR

⅛ TEASPOON SWEET PIMENTÓN (SPANISH SMOKED PAPRIKA)

1 TEASPOON SALT

1 TABLESPOON MINCED ONION

1 TABLESPOON MINCED FRESH FLAT-LEAF PARSLEY LEAVES

1 CUP FLAT MINERAL OR FILTERED WATER

¼ CUP VODKA

½ POUND FROZEN WHOLE TINY (1-INCH) SHRIMP, DEFROSTED

2 TEASPOONS COARSE SEA SALT

In a medium pot over medium-high heat, heat the olive oil until it measures 350°F on a candy thermometer. Sift the chickpea and all-purpose flours together in a mixing bowl, and season with the pimentón and salt. Add the onion and parsley to the flours and mix well. Slowly pour in the water and vodka, stirring constantly to prevent any lumps from forming. The mixture should be similar to a very thin pancake batter. Fold the shrimp into the batter.

Using a 3-ounce ladle, spoon the batter into the hot oil. The batter will begin to break apart in the oil. Using a slotted spoon, push the pieces of batter together against one side of the pot until the fritter begins to stick together. At this moment, turn the fritter over in the oil. Allow the fritter to fry until golden brown, about 3 minutes. Transfer the fritter to a paper towel–lined plate to drain. Sprinkle with sea salt and keep warm. Repeat with the remaining batter, making sure the oil returns to 350°F between batches. The batter will yield 10 to 12 fritters. Serve immediately.

José's Tip:
One-pound blocks of tiny shrimp can be found in Asian markets. You can substitute finely chopped peeled small shrimp, but add another cup of mineral water to the batter if you do so. Adding vodka to the batter helps the fritters turn out light and lacy.

Casa Balbino in Sanlúcar de Barrameda, in the province of Cadíz, is one of those restaurants I would love to work in. It should be a national monument. If you go there on a busy day and stand at the bar, you'll see why. There are people in shorts and people in suits, along with the hardworking (but smiling) servers. Waiting, you'll notice plates emerging from the kitchen piled high with crispy golden circles with baby shrimp; these are their famous tortilla de camarones. Look up on the wall and you'll see a board listing a number. The tortillas are so popular that you have to wait for your number to come up in order to get one. Try making them at home; they are one of the kings of Spanish tapas.

Gambas a la plancha

Shrimp cooked on a griddle

SERVES 4

1 POUND KOSHER SALT

16 MEDIUM SHRIMP, HEADS ON

Spread the salt on a flat griddle or in a medium frying pan and heat over medium-high heat. When the salt is hot, lay half the shrimp on the salt and cook for 3 to 4 minutes. Turn them over and cook for another 2 minutes. Transfer the shrimp to a serving platter and repeat with the remaining shrimp. Serve immediately.

You can cook this dish with shrimp from the Gulf of Mexico when they're in season. This is as simple a technique for cooking seafood as you'll ever find. The result is stunning—a perfect balance between the natural sweetness of the shrimp and the savory edge of the salt. I strongly recommend using the whole shrimp with their heads in their shells. That way you're sure to have juicy, flavorful shrimp.

Cigalas a la plancha

Norway lobster cooked on a griddle

SERVES 4

- 5 TEASPOONS SPANISH EXTRA-VIRGIN OLIVE OIL
- 8 (2-OUNCE) WHOLE CIGALAS (NORWAY LOBSTERS), SPLIT IN HALF LENGTHWISE
- JUICE OF ¼ LEMON (ABOUT 1 TEASPOON)
- COARSE SEA SALT TO TASTE
- ½ TEASPOON GRATED LEMON ZEST

On a flat griddle or in a medium frying pan, heat 1 teaspoon of the oil over medium-high heat. Place half the split lobsters on the griddle, shell side down, and cook without moving them for 3 minutes. Transfer the grilled lobsters to a warm serving platter and repeat with the remaining lobsters, adding another teaspoon of oil to the griddle.

Whisk together the remaining 3 teaspoons olive oil and the lemon juice. Spoon the dressing over the lobsters and sprinkle with salt and lemon zest.

A trip to Madrid's Chamartín market, a neighborhood market with wonderful seafood, inspired this dish. A griddle is perfect for this kind of seafood—a searing heat that cooks quickly without drying all the life out of the Norway lobster. Sometimes the freshest ingredients need a simple way of cooking.

Calamares con tinta romana

Squid fried with its ink

SERVES 4

4 LARGE FRESH SQUID, BODIES AND TENTACLES SEPARATED

1 EGG, BEATEN

1 TEASPOON SQUID INK

1 CUP PLUS 2 TABLESPOONS ALL-PURPOSE FLOUR

SALT TO TASTE

4 CUPS SPANISH EXTRA-VIRGIN OLIVE OIL

Rinse the squid under cold water and cut the bodies into ½-inch-thick rings. In a large bowl, combine the egg, squid ink, 1 cup flour, and 1 cup ice water and mix well with a wooden spoon, making sure to break up any lumps. The ink may be salty, so season the batter carefully with salt.

Heat the olive oil in a deep pot over medium-high heat until it measures 350°F on a candy thermometer. Lightly dust the squid with the remaining 2 tablespoons of flour. Working in batches, dip the squid in the batter, then carefully drop into the hot oil. Cook until crisp, about 2 minutes. Using a slotted spoon, transfer the squid to a paper towel-lined plate to drain. When the oil returns to 350°F, repeat with the remaining squid. Serve warm.

José's Tip:
Ice-cold batter yields puffy, crisp rings. Set the mixing bowl containing the batter in an ice bath while you fry the squid. Squid ink can be found in seafood shops or at the fish counter of your market.

El Bulli is a restaurant that means a lot to me. Ferran Adrià, his brother Albert (who is like a brother to me), and their partner, Juli Soler, are simply the best restaurant team in the world. Together they have earned worldwide acclaim for creating some of the most forward-thinking cooking of the last couple of centuries. But they are also masters of reinventing the classics. Here, Ferran starts out with traditional fried squid, which is very popular in Spain, then he gives it a new twist by bringing to the outside what is normally found on the inside of the squid: its ink.

Only in Spain could you make a movie called *Jamón, Jamón*, a romantic comedy in which ham is an expression of passion. Pork in all its forms—from smoky red chorizo sausage to translucent slices of cured ham—is a national obsession with a history dating to the fifteenth century. Under the Inquisition, when Jews and Muslims were massacred or expelled, a mere refusal to eat pork and ham was considered proof of heresy and a test for rooting out the Jews and Muslims who were trying to pass as Christians. Food was enough to send people to their death.

Today, few Spanish people need persuading to eat the extraordinary ham we call *Ibérico*, indisputably the finest (and most expensive) ham in the world. Ibérico ham is made from pure-bred black Iberian pigs, descendants of the wild boar, that live free-range on a diet of acorns. (The lower-quality Serrano ham is made from white pigs.) The acorns contribute to a meat that is layered with streaks of nutty-flavored fat that starts to melt at room temperature. This fat also makes the ham surprisingly healthy, with a chemical content of oleic acid that is similar to olive oil. From October to March, in woodlands and meadows across southwestern Spain, the pigs fatten up by devouring as much as 20 pounds of acorns each day. After slaughter, the hams are salted for three months, then dried for at least another three months. They are then hung in dark cellars for as long as two years to mature, developing the complex, rich flavor that is the meaty equivalent of a great red wine. For many years, burdensome government regulations kept this special ham out of the United States, but now you can buy it here in specialty stores and on the Web. It's worth ordering wherever you find it. Over the centuries, Spanish cooks have developed many ways to prepare pork, from sausages to meatballs, from pork loins to short ribs. The variety is surely a reflection of pork's intense history in Spain.

pork

cataluña

By the age of fifteen, I was enrolled in culinary school in Barcelona, where I had the freedom to do more than just study. Some of my best experience came very early in the morning, when I would go to the great Barcelona market known as La Boquería. I don't think there is a better way to understand a region or its gastronomy than visiting the local market. Inside La Boquería, you can sense the centuries of tradition. You can understand how Jews, Muslims, and Christians lived and traded together, bringing ingredients from distant parts of the world and creating this special bazaar.

As a kid who loved cooking from an early age, I was so fascinated by the place that I would sometimes show up before it opened. I would usually start the day spending whatever money I had at Pinotxo, the legendary market café where the owner, Juanito—always smiling and welcoming—would make his special café con leche with his old coffee machine. Each coffee, served in a tall glass, has perfectly separated layers of creamy milk on top and deep dark coffee below. Watching the line that separated the two liquids and the beautiful swirling waves that formed inside, I'd tell myself that some day I too would make coffee like Juanito. Next I would eat some ensaïmadas, small spiraled Majorcan pastries that are very popular in Barcelona. They would get perfectly caramelized on the plancha, or griddle, releasing the special flavor of pork fat that makes them such a delicacy.

There were other wonderful characters in the market too, like Llorenc Petras, who knows more about mushrooms than anyone alive. He looks like he just came out of the forest, and he knows where every mushroom grows. I was also fascinated by the great chef Isidre Gironés from Ca L'Isidre, who would shop for his restaurant trailed by an assistant whose job it was to ensure that every item got back to the restaurant safely. Each morning he would arrive in his perfect shirt and tie, often showing off the market to visitors from distant countries. One day I had the honor of sitting next to his daughter Nuria at Pinotxo, but I never talked to her because she was like aristocracy—the daughter of one of the most successful chefs in Barcelona. At the end of the afternoon, when the market was dying down, I always felt a sense of loss. I thought the market was in a sense a living thing that needed time to rest. So I would wait anxiously until the next morning, when it would come alive once again.

Catalonia is much more than the great market of La Boquería. Its olives are legendary, its cava wine is one of Spain's best exports, and the creativity the region fosters is extraordinary. There is the aromatic food in the mountains and the Mediterranean food of the coast. There are great sauces like the sofrito of onions and tomato and the samfaina stew of fresh vegetables. The bounty of local ingredients extends from fresh local seafood to great pork sausages called butifarra. Few regions boast more diversity and riches than Catalonia, a region that seems to inspire creativity. It's no coincidence that the same corner of Catalonia was home to Salvador Dalí as it is to my good friend, the avant-garde master chef Ferran Adrià.

Butifarra con setas

Catalan pork sausage with mushrooms

SERVES 4

1 POUND FRESH BUTIFARRA (MILD SPANISH PORK SAUSAGE)

¼ POUND CHANTERELLES OR OTHER WILD MUSHROOMS

1 TABLESPOON SPANISH EXTRA-VIRGIN OLIVE OIL

½ ONION, SLICED

¼ CUP MOSCATEL OR OTHER SWEET DESSERT WINE

2 FRESH THYME SPRIGS

1 BAY LEAF

2 TABLESPOONS RAISINS

2 TABLESPOONS PINE NUTS

SEA SALT TO TASTE

1 TABLESPOON CHOPPED FLAT-LEAF PARSLEY

Remove the sausage skins and cut the meat into 1-inch pieces. Slice the mushrooms in half or in quarters, depending on how large they are. The mushroom pieces should be about the same size so they cook evenly.

Heat the olive oil in a large sauté pan over medium-low heat. Add the sausage and brown on both sides, about 2 minutes. Using a slotted spoon or tongs, transfer the sausage to a plate. Add the onion to the pan and cook, stirring occasionally, until it is soft and golden brown, about 10 minutes. Pour in the Moscatel and reduce until the alcohol evaporates, about 30 seconds.

Increase the heat to medium, add the mushrooms, thyme, and bay leaf, and cook for another 2 minutes. Return the sausage to the pan, mix in the raisins and pine nuts, and cook for 2 more minutes. Season to taste with salt and garnish with parsley.

José's Tip:
Butifarra is available online and in specialty grocery stores. Substitute a mild pork sausage if you can't find it. In Catalonia, this sausage is often served with white beans—another great combination you can easily try at home.

Where I grew up in Catalonia, special holidays were often celebrated with a huge barbecue in the town square. Sizzling on the grills were hundreds and hundreds of sausages—butifarra—and the aroma as the fat dropped into the fire was overwhelming. They were the best hot dogs I ever tasted. Catalans love mushrooms almost as much as they love butifarra. There's no better combination than these two great Catalan ingredients.

Patatas con Chistorra "a mi manera"

Potato and chorizo "my way"

SERVES 4 TO 6

1 LARGE RUSSET POTATO, PEELED

4 CUPS SPANISH EXTRA-VIRGIN OLIVE OIL

8 OUNCES CHISTORRA CHORIZO (LONG, THIN BASQUE-STYLE SAUSAGE), CUT INTO 2-INCH PIECES

Using a mandoline, thinly slice the potato lengthwise. You need 20 of the largest slices; reserve the smaller slices for another use or discard (see tip). Put the potato slices in a bowl filled with ice water.

Heat the olive oil in a medium pot until it measures 325°F on a candy thermometer.

Remove a potato slice from the ice water and pat it dry with a paper towel. Lay the potato slice on a clean work surface and place a piece of chorizo in the center. Fold the potato slice over to form a half-moon. Pinch the slice closed around the chorizo and secure it by threading a toothpick through the edges of the potato. Repeat with the remaining potato slices and chorizo. You should have about 20 bundles.

Working in batches, fry the bundles until the potatoes are golden, about 3 minutes. Transfer to a paper towel to drain. Allow the oil to return to 325°F between batches.

Carefully remove the toothpicks while the bundles are still warm to prevent the potato slices from breaking. Keep warm until ready to serve.

I always find inspiration in the legendary dishes of my country and reinvent them "my way." Potatoes and chorizo is a classic combination in Spain; here I give these simple ingredients a modern twist.

José's Tip:
After you've fried all your potato and Chistorra bundles, fry the reserved smaller potato slices in the oil to make chips. Chistorra chorizo, a semi-cured cooking sausage flavored with lots of pimentón, can be found online and in specialty markets.

Albóndigas de cerdo con calamar

Pork meatballs with squid

SERVES 4

FOR THE MEATBALLS

1 SLICE DAY-OLD RUSTIC BREAD, CRUSTS REMOVED

3 TABLESPOONS WHOLE MILK, PLUS MORE IF NEEDED

1 POUND GROUND PORK

1 LARGE EGG

¼ TEASPOON GROUND CUMIN

1 TABLESPOON MINCED GARLIC

SEA SALT TO TASTE

FOR THE SAUCE

4 SMALL FRESH SQUID, CLEANED

3 GARLIC CLOVES, PEELED

1 TEASPOON SPANISH EXTRA-VIRGIN OLIVE OIL

1 FRESH THYME SPRIG

3 TABLESPOONS SOFRITO (PAGE 247)

2 TABLESPOONS DRY WHITE WINE

1 LARGE YUKON GOLD POTATO, PEELED AND CHOPPED

1 CINNAMON STICK

SEA SALT TO TASTE

1 CUP FLAT MINERAL OR FILTERED WATER, OR MORE IF NEEDED

1 CUP SPANISH EXTRA-VIRGIN OLIVE OIL

½ CUP ALL-PURPOSE FLOUR

1 TEASPOON CHOPPED PARSLEY

SEA SALT TO TASTE

Prepare the meatballs: Place the bread in a small bowl and pour enough of the milk over it to soften the bread. Combine the ground pork, milk-soaked bread, egg, cumin, and garlic in a large mixing bowl and season to taste with salt. Using your hands, mix the ingredients together until well combined, being careful not to overwork. Refrigerate the mixture for 1 hour.

Prepare the sauce: Lay the squid on a cutting board and separate the tentacles from the bodies with a sharp kitchen knife. Slice the squid bodies open and press them flat on the cutting board. Cut the squid bodies into thin strips and halve the tentacles.

Split open the garlic cloves by pressing down hard with the heel of your hand or the flat side of a kitchen knife. Heat the olive oil in a medium pot over medium heat. Add the garlic and cook for 2 minutes, then add the squid and cook for 5 minutes. Add the thyme, sofrito, and white wine and cook until the wine evaporates, about 3 minutes. Add the potatoes and cinnamon stick and season to taste with salt. Add the mineral water and cook for 15 to 20 minutes, or until the potatoes are tender. Make sure to add more water if necessary to keep the potatoes covered while cooking. Season to taste with more salt, cover, and set aside.

Roll the chilled meat mixture into balls, using 1½ tablespoons for each ball, between the palms of your hands (you should end up with 16 meatballs). Heat the cup of olive oil in a medium pot until it measures 325°F on a candy thermometer. Working in batches, gently toss the meatballs in the flour, making sure to shake off any excess flour, then fry the meatballs until browned, about 2 minutes. Using a slotted spoon, transfer the meatballs to a paper towel–lined plate to drain. Allow the oil to return to 325°F between batches.

Return the sauce to the stovetop and heat over low heat. Add the meatballs and cook for 8 to 10 minutes or until the meatballs are firm to the touch. Add more water if the sauce begins to evaporate. Divide the meatballs and squid tentacles between 4 plates and spoon remaining sauce over meatballs. Garnish with chopped parsley, and season to taste with salt.

Like so many other Spanish words, *albóndigas* starts with "al," which means it is a remnant of the Muslim influence on our language—and our cooking. Every culture seems to have some kind of ground meat dish, and Spain is no different, only here the meatball is made of pork, not beef—another sign of Spain's conversion from Muslim to Christian rule.

Fideua con costillas de cerdo y cigalas

Noodle paella with pork short ribs and Norwegian lobsters

SERVES 4 TO 6

FOR THE STOCK

6 CIGALAS (NORWEGIAN LOBSTERS), OR LARGE HEAD-ON SHRIMP

1 TABLESPOON SPANISH EXTRA-VIRGIN OLIVE OIL

½ HEAD GARLIC, PAPERY OUTER SKIN REMOVED, BROKEN INTO CLOVES

½ ONION, PEELED

1 BAY LEAF

1 TEASPOON BLACK PEPPERCORNS

FOR THE PICADA VERDE

1 SMALL GARLIC CLOVE, PEELED

¼ CUP FRESH FLAT-LEAF PARSLEY LEAVES

PINCH OF SALT

1 TABLESPOON SPANISH EXTRA-VIRGIN OLIVE OIL

FOR THE PASTA

2 TABLESPOONS SPANISH EXTRA-VIRGIN OLIVE OIL

2 CUPS FIDEOS (VERY SHORT FINE SPANISH NOODLES) OR 8 OUNCES ANGEL HAIR PASTA, BROKEN INTO 1-INCH PIECES

1-POUND SLAB BABY BACK RIBS, HALVED LENGTHWISE AND SEPARATED INTO RIBLETS

SEA SALT TO TASTE

½ CUP SALMORRA (PAGE 248)

⅛ TEASPOON SWEET PIMENTÓN (SPANISH SMOKED PAPRIKA)

José's Tip:

If you don't have a paella pan, use a large sauté pan instead.

While we usually associate pasta with Italy, Spain also has great pasta dishes, as this recipe demonstrates. The pasta cooks, like a paella, by soaking up a special tasty stock. The result is unlike any pasta you're used to eating at home or in an Italian restaurant.

Prepare the stock: Pull the heads off of the cigalas and set the tails aside. Heat the olive oil in a medium pot over medium-high heat and add the heads and the garlic. Using a wooden spoon or potato masher, crush the heads and sauté them with the garlic until they turn red. Add 2 quarts of water, the onion, bay leaf, and peppercorns. Bring to a boil over high heat, then reduce the heat to low and simmer for 45 minutes, skimming any foam that forms on top. Strain the stock through a fine-mesh strainer into a small pot, discarding the solids. Keep the stock hot over low heat.

For the picada: Using a mortar and pestle, mash the garlic clove, parsley, and a pinch of salt into a paste. Drizzle in the olive oil as you continue to mash until the oil is well combined. Set aside.

Preheat the broiler.

Prepare the pasta: Heat the olive oil in a 13-inch paella pan over medium heat, add the pasta and sauté until toasted and golden brown, 5 to 6 minutes. Spoon the pasta into a bowl and set aside. Increase the heat to medium-high and sear the reserved cigalas tails on each side in the same pan. Remove the tails to a plate and set aside. Season the ribs with salt, then arrange the ribs in the same pan and sear them on each side, about 2 minutes per side. Push the ribs to the edge of the pan and reduce the heat to medium Add the salmorra to the paella pan and sauté for 1 minute. Push the ribs back to the center of the pan and toss with the salmorra, cooking for 3 more minutes. Add the toasted pasta and stir until well combined. Sprinkle with the pimentón, then pour in 3½ cups of the reserved hot stock. Season to taste with salt and cook over medium heat for 8 minutes. Reduce the heat to low. Split the cigalas tails in half with a sharp kitchen knife and add to the pan, shell side down, and cook for 2 more minutes.

Put the pan under the broiler and cook until the pasta on the surface starts to curl up and brown slightly, about 2 minutes. Remove the paella pan from the oven and drizzle with the picada verde.

Lomo de cerdo asado en sal con Jamón

Pork loin baked in sea salt with sliced Spanish cured ham

SERVES 4 TO 6

3 POUNDS SEA SALT

4 SPRIGS FRESH ROSEMARY

4 SPRIGS FRESH FLAT-LEAF PARSLEY

6 SPRIGS FRESH THYME

1 2-POUND PORK LOIN

4 OUNCES THINLY SLICED JAMÓN SERRANO (SPANISH CURED HAM)

SPANISH EXTRA-VIRGIN OLIVE OIL

Preheat the oven to 400°F.

In a large bowl, mix the salt with 3 tablespoons water until the salt is slightly damp. (The salt must be moist so it will pack well.) Spread half of the salt down the center of a baking sheet and top with 2 rosemary sprigs, 2 parsley sprigs, and 3 thyme sprigs. Lay the pork loin on top of the herbs. Place the remaining herbs on top of the pork, then cover the pork completely with the remaining salt, making sure to pack it well around the pork. Bake for 25 minutes.

Let the pork rest for 5 minutes. Using a fork and spoon, crack open the side of the salt crust. The upper half of the crust, now a hard shell, should lift off easily. Transfer the pork to a cutting board and let rest for another 5 minutes. Slice the loin into ½-inch-thick slices and arrange on 4 plates. Lay slices of the jamón between the pork slices. Drizzle with olive oil and serve warm.

José's Tip:
This is an easy and delicious cooking technique for meats and fish.

Santiago Martín produces Ibérico ham in one of the most beautiful towns in Spain—La Alberca, in the province of Salamanca. He was the first person to export Ibérico ham to Japan and the United States. He's also a great host. One day I was visiting his factory and I saw a loin of ham, marbled with delicious acorn-infused fat, and a big pile of the salt they used for curing. I suggested cooking the loin for his family, baking it over a charcoal fire on a bed of salt. We put the loin on the salt and covered it with more salt to protect it from the hot coals. Around 40 minutes later, the loin was perfectly cooked. I sliced it and tucked pieces of cured ham between the cuts of loin. It was delicious—and tasted even better with all the great Spanish wine we drank.

castilla y león

My friend Magín Revillo is from León, and he makes an astonishing garlic soup using just white bread, garlic, and pimentón. You need to be a very good cook to achieve such brilliant results from so little. Magín and his wife, Nuria, spent many years hosting a popular Spanish radio show where they would travel around the country talking about an overlooked part of Spain—and they often showcased regional foods. One place Magín always talked about was a nameless restaurant in León, to which he made an annual pilgrimage. To stand any chance of admission, you needed someone to recommend you to the owner. The place would seat just one party a day, no more—whether it was five or ten or fifty people. I guess they don't like to handle more than one check at a time in León.

That's the character of Castilla y León: uncomplicated, taking the time to savor life one bite at a time. The region is famous for its cocido maragato, a meat-and-vegetable stew that is eaten in a very distinctive way. Elsewhere, people eat their cocido by starting with soup and ending with the meat and vegetables. In León, they do it the other way around—starting with the meat and ending with the soup. According to the locals, the best explanation for this tradition is that their forefathers needed the protein before rushing out to battle. That may be because the region, northwest of Madrid, was often at war. For centuries it was fought over, first by Christians and Muslims during the Reconquest, then by rival noblemen in the region. After all, this is the home of the great romantic hero El Cid, and castles and fortresses dot the landscape.

The region's farmland is dominated by cereal crops and beans, but its best product is its livestock; from the Ibérico hams of Guijuelo to the baby lambs and pigs that are a specialty of its great wood-oven restaurants. With a dish of roast suckling pig and a bottle of the region's wonderful Ribera del Duero wine, you have a meal that's worth fighting for.

When you see all the hams hanging in a Spanish market or bar, you might find it hard to believe other meats are used in Spanish cooking at all. But some of the most traditional dishes in Spain have nothing to do with pigs. Spain's name is itself a clue: The word *Hispania* means "the land of rabbits," so named by the Carthaginians, who found rabbits everywhere they traveled in our country. Rabbit still features in rice dishes in the east, and other meats, such as pheasant, are also used in rural areas, where hunting remains a popular pastime. There are classic lamb roasts in Aragón and Castilla, and satisfying chicken empanadas in Galicia. With all the wonderful dairy cows in northern Spain, it's only natural to find great beef dishes there too, often simply grilled over charcoal. Far from being narrow in their tastes, Spaniards like to eat every type of meat they can find.

other meats

aragón

I was eight years old when I first traveled to Aragón in northern Spain to visit an elderly uncle of my father's. I remember driving to an old house in Puebla de Valverde, where my father was born. It was still a time when people lived by the day and the night, the sun and the moon. We arrived late in the afternoon, just after the last rays of the sun had sunk behind the mountains, and my uncle was cooking for us. An old wooden table that looked like it had seen many wars and battles stood before a giant chimney that a little boy like me could fit inside. Inside the fireplace was a big old iron pan filled with simple ingredients like stale bread that he had cut up with an old penknife. He was cooking migas, which literally means "crumbs." He added some pork fat, garlic, and herbs. After 30 or 40 minutes, the crumbs were perfectly toasted on the outside and semisoft on the inside, with the aroma of the old, slightly rancid pork fat. They were so delectable I probably ate two or three plates. I never had migas like those again, and I probably never will—not only because the dish was new to me then but because it was made by a very special person in a very special place.

Aragón is famous in Spain for simple, rustic dishes like these: Lamb is roasted with potatoes or served in stews. Partridges are cooked with cabbage. And there's the classic dish pollo al chilindrón, chicken with vegetables grown in the fertile Ebro River plain.

I soon learned what the people of Aragón have known for centuries—to enjoy the delicious ingredients they find all around them. A couple of years after that first visit, we returned to Huesca in Aragón. We stopped at the Monasterio de Piedra, an unusual monastery surround by acres of beautiful land, covered with trees and waterfalls—including one spectacular waterfall called Cola de Caballo. Most people walk along a path to get there, but I'm not able to follow paths, and my unorthodox route led me to a field of wild strawberries that called to me with their wonderful red color. The sweetness of those strawberries remains vivid to me still, reminding me that, in life, it doesn't matter whether you're searching for something—all you have to do is be ready for discovery.

Empanada de pollo

Galician-style chicken turnover

SERVES 4 TO 6

FOR THE FILLING

- 1 3-POUND CHICKEN
- SEA SALT AND FRESHLY CRACKED BLACK PEPPER TO TASTE
- ½ CUP SPANISH EXTRA-VIRGIN OLIVE OIL
- 1 GREEN BELL PEPPER, SEEDED AND THINLY SLICED
- 1 RED BELL PEPPER, SEEDED AND THINLY SLICED
- 3 MEDIUM SPANISH ONIONS, THINLY SLICED
- 4 GARLIC CLOVES, MINCED
- 8 RIPE PLUM TOMATOES
- 1 FRESH THYME SPRIG
- 2 BAY LEAVES
- ½ CUP DRY WHITE WINE, SUCH AS ALBARIÑO
- 2 TEASPOONS SWEET PIMENTÓN (SPANISH SMOKED PAPRIKA)

FOR THE DOUGH

- 1½ TEASPOONS ACTIVE DRY YEAST
- PINCH OF SUGAR
- 3 CUPS ALL-PURPOSE FLOUR, PLUS MORE FOR DUSTING
- 2 TEASPOONS SALT
- ¼ TEASPOON SWEET PIMENTÓN (SPANISH SMOKED PAPRIKA)
- ⅓ CUP FLAT MINERAL OR FILTERED WATER
- ½ TEASPOON SPANISH EXTRA-VIRGIN OLIVE OIL, PLUS MORE FOR THE BAKING SHEET
- 1 LARGE EGG

Preheat the oven to 375°F.

Prepare the filling: Season the chicken inside and out with salt and pepper and place on a rack set on top of a baking sheet. Roast the chicken for 45 minutes and let cool. Remove all of the meat from the chicken, discarding the skin and bones. Shred the meat and set aside.

Heat the olive oil in a medium saucepan over medium-low heat. Add the peppers, onions, and garlic and cook, stirring occasionally, until the onions and peppers are tender and golden brown, about 30 minutes. Meanwhile, slice the tomatoes in half. Place a grater over a mixing bowl. Rub the cut surface of the tomatoes over the grater until all of the flesh is grated. Set the pulp aside and discard the skins.

Add the thyme and bay leaves to the onions and peppers and continue to cook until the mixture turns brown, about 5 minutes more. Add the wine and cook until it evaporates. Stir in the tomato pulp and pimentón, increase the heat to medium, and cook slowly until the oil separates from the mixture and the tomato becomes dark brown in color, about 20 minutes more. Add the shredded chicken and cook for 5 more minutes. Remove from the heat and discard the bay leaves. Season to taste with salt. Transfer the mixture to a strainer set over a mixing bowl and let cool, reserving the liquid that drains off.

This recipe can be simplified by using puff pastry in place of the empanada dough, but to me that's like mixing the aristocratic with the humble. Puff pastry is so refined. The real empanada—the food of the humble pilgrim on the way to Santiago de Compostela—is more basic and comforting. If you have the time, be authentic and make your own dough.

Prepare the dough: Dissolve the yeast and sugar in 1 tablespoon warm water. Mix the flour, salt, and pimentón together in the bowl of a standing mixer fitted with a dough hook. Add the yeast mixture and mix on low speed. Slowly drizzle in the mineral water and 4 tablespoons of the reserved liquid from the filling. Increase the speed to medium and mix until the dough forms a ball. If the dough does not come together, add 1 or 2 tablespoons water. The dough should be slightly sticky. Oil a mixing bowl with ½ teaspoon of olive oil. Put the dough into the bowl, cover with a clean kitchen towel, and set aside to rise for 1 hour.

Preheat the oven to 400°F. Turn the dough out onto a lightly floured surface and knead gently to deflate it. Form the dough back into a ball and cut it into 2 equal halves. Dust the work surface with a little more flour. With a rolling pin, roll each piece into an 11 x 9-inch rectangle, about 1/4 inch thick. Lightly brush the back of a baking sheet with the oil. Transfer 1 rectangle of dough to the baking sheet. Spoon the filling into the center of the dough and spread to about 1 inch from the edge. Beat the egg in a small bowl with a little water and brush the egg wash along the edge of the dough. Place the second rectangle of dough on top of the filling. Fold the dough over, crimping the edges to seal. Brush the top of the dough with egg wash and prick with a fork to allow the steam to escape. Bake until golden brown, about 30 minutes. Allow the empanada to come to room temperature before slicing.

José's Tip:
You can use 1/4-inch-thick sheets of puff pastry if you don't want to make the dough, but it will lack the wonderful flavor that comes from using the liquid infused with the filling. Instead of roasting your own chicken, you could simply buy a good-quality roast chicken from your local supermarket.

Alas de pollo confitadas con puré de aceitunas verdes

Chicken wing confit with green olive purée

SERVES 4

4½ CUPS PLUS 2 TABLESPOONS SPANISH EXTRA-VIRGIN OLIVE OIL

7 GARLIC CLOVES, 3 CLOVES PEELED AND MINCED

8 FRESH THYME SPRIGS

½ TEASPOON SWEET PIMENTÓN (SPANISH SMOKED PAPRIKA)

1½ POUNDS CHICKEN WINGLETS (UPPER JOINT ONLY), ABOUT 12 PIECES

SEA SALT TO TASTE

¼ CUP TIGHTLY PACKED FRESH FLAT-LEAF PARSLEY LEAVES

½ CUP PITTED GREEN OLIVES

¼ CUP FLAT MINERAL OR FILTERED WATER

3 FRESH ROSEMARY SPRIGS

1 BAY LEAF

2 CUPS DRY BREADCRUMBS

José's Tip:
Note that the wings must marinate overnight.

Combine 2 tablespoons of the olive oil, the minced garlic, 5 sprigs of thyme, and the pimentón in a large mixing bowl. Add the chicken winglets, toss to coat, and season with salt. Cover the bowl with plastic wrap and refrigerate overnight.

In a blender, combine the parsley, olives, ¼ cup of the olive oil, and the mineral water and blend until smooth. Heat 4 cups of the olive oil in a large, wide pot over low heat until it measures 200°F on a candy thermometer. Add the remaining 4 garlic cloves, 2 rosemary sprigs, 2 thyme sprigs, and the bay leaf to the oil. Add the winglets, spreading them out in the pot so they cook evenly. Cook for 20 minutes or until the meat starts to separate from the bones. Transfer the winglets to a paper towel-lined plate and drain. When cool enough to handle, carefully debone the winglets with your fingers, trying to keep their shape.

Remove the leaves from the remaining rosemary and thyme sprigs and chop finely. Combine the herbs with the breadcrumbs in a large mixing bowl. Add the winglets and pat them with the breadcrumbs, making sure to coat them well. Heat the remaining ¼ cup olive oil in a large sauté pan (the oil should cover the bottom of the pan) over medium heat. Working in batches, carefully add the breaded winglets to the pan and cook until golden brown on both sides, about 4 minutes total. Transfer the breaded winglets to a paper towel-lined plate to drain.

Top winglets with the olive purée and season with salt.

Humble and inexpensive chicken wings get the royal treatment when prepared as a confit. The olive purée makes for a great combination with the chicken confit. In fact, it's so good you'll want to pair it with lots of other dishes too.

Pollo al chilindrón

Chicken with peppers, tomatoes, onions, and Spanish ham

SERVES 4

¼ CUP SPANISH EXTRA-VIRGIN OLIVE OIL, PLUS 1 TABLESPOON

4 CHICKEN LEGS, THIGHS AND DRUMSTICKS SEPARATED

SALT TO TASTE

2 CUPS DICED SPANISH ONIONS

½ CUP DICED GREEN BELL PEPPERS

½ CUP DICED RED BELL PEPPERS

2 TABLESPOONS MINCED GARLIC

1 CUP DRY WHITE WINE

½ CUP THINLY SLICED AND DICED JAMÓN SERRANO (SPANISH CURED HAM)

½ TEASPOON SWEET PIMENTÓN (SPANISH SMOKED PAPRIKA)

2 CUPS PLAIN CANNED TOMATO SAUCE

1 FRESH ROSEMARY SPRIG

1 BAY LEAF

2 CUPS FLAT MINERAL OR FILTERED WATER

Heat 1 tablespoon of the olive oil in a 12-quart pot over medium-high heat. Season the chicken pieces with salt. Working in batches, brown them on all sides. Transfer the chicken to a platter and set aside.

Add ¼ cup olive oil to the same pot and, when the oil is hot, add the onions and peppers. Reduce the heat to low and cook slowly until the vegetables are dark golden brown, about 30 minutes. Add 1 tablespoon water if the onions start to burn. Add the garlic and cook for 5 more minutes. Add the white wine and cook until it evaporates, 4 to 5 minutes.

Add the jamón and browned chicken pieces, as well as any juices that have collected, and cook for 5 more minutes. Stir in the pimentón, tomato sauce, rosemary, bay leaf, and the mineral water and simmer over low heat for 1 hour or until the meat starts to fall off the bone. Season to taste with salt before serving.

Chilindrón is a wonderful vegetable stew that comes from Aragón, where they grow astonishing vegetables in the fertile land near the Ebro River. This dish is a traditional combination with chicken, which makes for a great family dinner. Just remember not to rush the cooking here. When cooked low and slow, the sweetness from the onions, peppers, and pimentón is memorable.

Solomillo con queso Picón

Beef tenderloin with Picón cheese

SERVES 4

2 TEASPOONS SPANISH EXTRA-VIRGIN OLIVE OIL

1 POUND BEEF TENDERLOIN

3 GARLIC CLOVES, PEELED

½ SHALLOT, THINLY SLICED

2 FRESH THYME SPRIGS

¼ CUP SIDRA (SPANISH HARD CIDER) OR OTHER HIGH-QUALITY HARD CIDER

½ CUP HEAVY CREAM

2 OUNCES PICÓN (SPANISH BLUE CHEESE FROM CANTABRIA) OR OTHER GOOD-QUALITY BLUE CHEESE

SEA SALT TO TASTE

CHOPPED CHIVES

José's Tip:
If you can't find Picón cheese, use another blue cheese you like, such as a good Stilton.

Preheat the oven to 450°F. Heat the olive oil in a large ovenproof sauté pan over high heat. When the oil begins to smoke, add the tenderloin and sear on all sides, about 2 minutes per side. Transfer the pan to the oven and cook the tenderloin for 10 minutes or until it measures 130°F on a meat thermometer (for medium rare). Transfer the tenderloin to a platter and keep warm.

Carefully return the sauté pan to the stovetop and heat over medium-high heat. Gently crush the garlic cloves with the flat side of a kitchen knife and add them to the pan along with the shallot and thyme. Cook for 2 minutes, then add the sidra and 2 tablespoons water to deglaze the pan, scraping up any brown bits. Reduce the heat to medium and stir in the cream and 1 ounce of the Picón cheese. Keep stirring as the cheese melts into the sauce and the sauce begins to thicken. Remove the pan from the heat and set aside.

Slice the tenderloin into ½-inch-thick medallions and arrange on 4 plates. Season with salt and spoon the cheese sauce over and around the medallions. Crumble the remaining 1 ounce Picón cheese over the medallions and garnish with chives.

It seems as if every great blue cheese is paired with a great meat. There's something irresistible about the combination of tangy, pungent cheese and good-quality, soft red meat. Here we use a Cantabrian cheese called Picón with a great juicy beef tenderloin to make a very satisfying meal.

Cordero asado con patatas

Roasted rack of lamb with potatoes

SERVES 4

4 YUKON GOLD POTATOES, PEELED AND CUT INTO 1/4-INCH-THICK ROUNDS

8 GARLIC CLOVES, PEELED

16 PEARL ONIONS, PEELED

4 FRESH ROSEMARY SPRIGS

4 FRESH THYME SPRIGS

3 TABLESPOONS SPANISH EXTRA-VIRGIN OLIVE OIL

SEA SALT TO TASTE

2 FRENCH-CUT RACKS OF LAMB, ABOUT 10 OUNCES EACH

1/2 CUP DRY WHITE WINE

Preheat the oven to 450°F.

Toss the potato slices, garlic, onions, rosemary, thyme, and 1 tablespoon of the olive oil together in a mixing bowl. Spread the mixture in a large roasting pan, season to taste with salt, and bake in the oven for 10 minutes.

While the potatoes roast, heat 1 tablespoon of the olive oil in a large sauté pan over medium-high heat. When the pan begins to smoke, add the lamb racks and brown about 2 minutes per side.

Remove the potatoes from the oven and pour the wine over them. Arrange the lamb racks on top of the potatoes, leaning them against each other to form a triangle. Return the pan to the oven and cook for another 20 minutes or until the lamb measures 130°F on a meat thermometer. Transfer the lamb to a cutting board to let rest for 5 minutes.

Slice the racks into chops and divide them among 4 plates. Spoon the potatoes, onions, garlic, and herbs onto the plates. Drizzle the lamb with the pan juices and the remaining tablespoon of olive oil. Season to taste with salt.

José's Tip:
If your lamb racks weigh more than 10 ounces, they will take longer to cook. Be sure to watch the potatoes to make sure they don't burn.

This classic dish from Aragón is found in many of the region's great roasting restaurants. I started cooking it for my Jewish friends in the United States for their Passover meal, not least because lamb plays a symbolic role during their holiday feast. In any religion, on either side of the Atlantic, this is a simple and satisfying meal the whole family can enjoy.

To say that Spaniards enjoy their sweets is an understatement. Spanish people eat sweet pastries and dishes in the morning, afternoon, and evening. There are churros, fried strips of dough, for breakfast. There's the creamy rice and milk dessert called arroz con leche that is so popular in my home region of Asturias. And there are the wonderfully rich egg-based sweets produced by the nuns of Andalusia—a throwback to the days when the sherry-makers would clarify their wines with egg whites and donate the yolks to the convents. Many of our best sweets are legacies of the even older culture of the Moors. Each Christmas, Spanish families give one another turrón, a slab of honey, sugar, egg white, and toasted almonds. The almonds and honey are (ironically for a Christmas gift) a typically Moorish combination. Turrón comes in two forms: the soft, light brown style made in Jijona and the pale, hard type popular in Alicante. Marzipan pastries are found all over Catalonia in the north and Andalusia in the south. So you can enjoy the sweet tastes of Spain wherever you travel across the country—and of course make them at home.

sweets

FABA
EXTR
EL MUSEO DEL QUESO
Especialidad en:
Anchoas de Santoña
Bonito del Norte
Ventresca de Bonito
Quesadas del día
Bizcochos Caseros
Sobaos con Miel
Corbatas de Unquera
Pejinas (con cabello de ángel)
Orujo de Potes Natural
artesanas de Cantabria
Mermeladas
Mieles
SIDRA DE ASTURIAS
DENOMINACIÓN DE ORIGEN
QUESO CABRALES
12'95
EUROS
KILO
P.V.P.

asturias

I have a love affair with Asturias, the region I called home for the first five years of my life. I left Oviedo, the capital, when my father took a job in Barcelona in the early 1970s. At that time, Spain was still recovering from the civil war and going through the last years of the Franco regime. Traveling 1,000 kilometers was no minor task, and it wasn't easy to return to your home region once you left. The first stories I remember are those my mother and father told about our family back in Asturias.

To many people in Spain, Asturias is known for its changeable weather. There aren't many places where rainy skies can give way to a sunny day in a matter of minutes, as they do in Asturias. To some people, this may be a bad thing, but to me, it's one of the reasons I feel alive every time I'm in Asturias.

I still have a strong recollection of the first time I went back to the small town in Asturias where I was born. My father put me on a train that left Barcelona early in the evening and arrived the next morning in Mieres. I was maybe twelve or thirteen years old. I remember the family on my mother's side, picture-perfect, waiting for me at the station. And I clearly remember the aromas at the train station: the coal of the trains, the beautiful green trees, the sea air from the waves crashing against the rocks.

But the most vivid memories for me are, as always, food-related, like the fabada asturiana, the wonderful bean stew of the region, or the pungency of the Cabrales blue cheese. Food is always celebrated in Asturias; it doesn't matter how much it cost or how little there is on the table. Meals are times for everyone to share their stories of the past, the present, and the future. I loved listening to my cousins and my uncles talk about my grandfather Ramón. I still think I can remember him talking to me, though it was my grandmother Carlota who inspired me to become a cook. (At that time, in that culture, she would never let her husband get close to the kitchen unless he was bringing her pheasants or fish he had caught himself.)

Whenever I have a few free hours in Spain, I drive or take a plane to see my family in Asturias, and while there, I always spend some time in a sidrería. I love the sound of the cider splashing into a beautiful glass from high above the head of the escanciador (the special cider pourer). I love the bubbles that last for just a few seconds in the cider, which you have to drink in one big gulp before the air disappears. And I dream of Asturia's wonderful desserts, like a creamy arroz con leche, made with Spanish rice and fresh milk from Asturian cows. That alone makes it worth the travel time.

Tortitas de aceite de oliva

Olive oil pancakes

SERVES 4

- 1¾ CUPS ALL-PURPOSE FLOUR
- 2 TABLESPOONS SUGAR
- 2 TEASPOONS BAKING POWDER
- ½ TEASPOON BAKING SODA
- ¼ TEASPOON SALT
- 1 EGG, LIGHTLY BEATEN
- 1½ CUPS BUTTERMILK
- 4 TABLESPOONS SPANISH EXTRA-VIRGIN OLIVE OIL, PLUS MORE IF NECESSARY
- ⅓ CUP DARK CHOCOLATE, PREFERABLY SPANISH, BROKEN INTO SMALL PIECES
- ¼ CUP HONEY, PREFERABLY SPANISH LEMON HONEY
- FRESH MINT LEAVES

Mix the flour, sugar, baking powder, baking soda, and salt together in a mixing bowl. Whisk in the egg, buttermilk, and 2 tablespoons of the olive oil until you have a smooth batter, then stir in the chocolate pieces.

Heat the remaining 2 tablespoons of olive oil in a medium sauté pan over medium-low heat. Ladle ¼ cup of the pancake mixture into the pan and cook until golden brown. Flip the pancake with a spatula and cook until golden brown on the second side. Transfer the pancake to a warm oven. Repeat with the remaining batter, adding more olive oil to the pan as needed. To serve, drizzle the pancakes with honey and garnish with mint.

I love making these pancakes with my daughters, who adore the chocolate that makes them special. As for me, I appreciate the healthy qualities of this recipe. Once you are in on the secret that you can make pancakes with healthy olive oil, why would you ever want to use butter again?

José's Tip:
These pancakes are a perfect showcase for some of Spain's most delicious products—olive oil, chocolate, and honey—so be sure to seek them out in specialty markets.

Fresas con vino de Madrid

Strawberries with Madrid wine, herbs, and orange zest

SERVES 4

- 2 CUPS SPICY RED WINE, PREFERABLY A TEMPRANILLO FROM MADRID
- 4 TABLESPOONS SUGAR
- 1 BAY LEAF
- ZEST OF 1 LEMON
- ZEST OF 1 ORANGE
- 1 CINNAMON STICK
- FRESHLY CRACKED BLACK PEPPER
- 1 PINT FRESH STRAWBERRIES, HULLED AND HALVED
- FRESH MINT LEAVES
- FRESH EDIBLE FLOWERS (OPTIONAL)

In a medium saucepan, combine the wine, sugar, bay leaf, lemon and orange zests, cinnamon stick, and a couple of grindings of pepper from a pepper mill. Bring to a boil over high heat, then reduce the heat to low and simmer until the mixture is reduced by two-thirds, about 20 minutes. The syrup should have the consistency of honey and coat the back of a spoon. Strain the syrup through a fine-mesh strainer, discarding the solids. Spoon the strawberries into bowls and drizzle with the syrup. Garnish with mint leaves and edible flowers, if you like.

When we visited the royal town of Aranjuez for the TV show, we looked at the palace, of course. But the place I enjoyed the most was the strawberry farm, where we sampled the town's most famous and deliciously sweet fruit.

Manzanas con vino de La Rioja

Apples in La Rioja wine

SERVES 4

1 CUP SUGAR

4 CUPS DRY RED WINE, PREFERABLY FROM RIOJA

1 CUP TOP-QUALITY BRANDY, PREFERABLY CARDENAL MENDOZA

1 CINNAMON STICK

1 BAY LEAF

1 FRESH ROSEMARY SPRIG

1 FRESH THYME SPRIG

2 GRANNY SMITH OR GOLDEN DELICIOUS APPLES

1 QUART VANILLA ICE CREAM (OPTIONAL)

Combine the sugar, wine, brandy, cinnamon stick, bay leaf, rosemary, and thyme in a medium pot. Bring to a boil, then reduce the heat to low and simmer until the mixture is reduced to about 1 cup, about 30 minutes. The syrup's consistency should resemble honey and coat the back of your spoon. Strain the syrup, discarding the solids, and return the syrup to the pot.

Peel the apples and use a melon baller to scoop out balls, about 10 balls per apple. Reheat the wine syrup over low heat and add the apple balls. Simmer until the apples are cooked through and can be pierced easily with a toothpick, about 5 minutes. Divide the warm apples and syrup among 4 bowls and top with vanilla ice cream, if you like.

This is a wonderfully sweet and aromatic dessert, where the fresh apples are infused with a thick wine syrup. Just make sure the wine you cook with isn't inferior in quality; it should be a wine you would drink on its own. You'll get the best results with your cooking if you use the best possible ingredients—such as the high-quality La Rioja wine I recommend.

José's Tip:
Be sure to use a good-quality brandy for this syrup. Cardenal Mendoza is a brandy from Jerez that has been made in Spain for over 120 years. Mixed with the Rioja wine, this rich syrup offers a special flavor of Spain.

Postre de turrón

Almond nougat dessert

SERVES 4

- 3 LARGE EGG YOLKS
- 1/3 CUP SUGAR
- 1 CUP WHOLE MILK
- 1 1/4 TEASPOONS UNFLAVORED GELATIN POWDER
- 12 OUNCES JIJONA TURRÓN (SOFT SPANISH NOUGAT)
- 1/2 CUP HEAVY CREAM
- 1/4 CUP CHOPPED MARCONA ALMONDS
- SEA SALT TO TASTE
- 4 TABLESPOONS HONEY, PREFERABLY SPANISH

Whisk the egg yolks, sugar, and milk together in a medium pot until creamy in texture. Heat the milk mixture over medium-low heat until it reaches 185°F on a candy thermometer. Stir continuously with a spatula to keep the egg from sticking to the sides and bottom of the pot. Remove the pot from the heat and stir in the gelatin until it dissolves.

Crumble 11 ounces of the turrón in a large mixing bowl. Pour the milk mixture through a fine-mesh strainer into the mixing bowl. Using an immersion blender, blend the mixture with the turrón until smooth, about 2 minutes. Set aside to cool completely, about 30 minutes.

Meanwhile, in another large mixing bowl, whip the cream until stiff peaks form. Gently fold the whipped cream into the cooled turrón mixture. Do not whip or stir. Spoon the mixture into a square baking dish. Refrigerate for 30 minutes, covered with plastic wrap to prevent a skin from forming.

To serve, place large spoonfuls of the mixture onto plates and, using a vegetable peeler, shave the remaining turrón over the tops. Sprinkle with almonds and sea salt and drizzle with honey.

Christmas in Spain is synonymous with turrón, a Spanish nougat made from almonds and honey. We all give one another big boxes of turrón, so we're always looking for ways to use it up before the next Christmas comes around. Here we've transformed the sweet from a December dish into a summer one. By the way, you can sprinkle crumbled turrón on top of a salad for extra flavor and texture—should you still have some left over.

José's Tip:
Turrón comes in one of two types: Alicante, a hard brittle texture, and Jijona, a softer nougat. For this recipe you want to use the Jijona variety.

Yogur de sferificacion con clementinas

Spherification of yogurt with clementines

SERVES 4

FOR THE SPHERIFICATION

1 TEASPOON ALGINATE

4¼ CUPS FLAT MINERAL OR FILTERED WATER

½ CUP PLAIN YOGURT

1½ TEASPOONS SUGAR

6 CLEMENTINES

4 TABLESPOONS HONEY, PREFERABLY SPANISH

¼ CUP SWEET MUSCAT WINE, PREFERABLY FROM ALICANTE

¼ CUP FRESH MINT LEAVES

José's Tip:

This recipe may seem difficult, but once you learn the technique you will be amazing your friends and family. The alginate can be found online, and I recommend using the Texturas brand from my friend Ferran Adrià.

Prepare the spherification: Put the alginate and 2 cups of the mineral water in a blender and blend for 1 minute at medium speed. Pour the liquid into a small square baking dish and refrigerate for 2 hours.

Combine the yogurt, sugar, and ¼ cup of the mineral water in a bowl. Using a deep, rounded teaspoon (like a measuring spoon), take a spoonful of the sweetened yogurt and carefully slide it into the alginated water without submerging the spoon in the water. (The spoon should barely touch the surface of the water.) A round ball will form once the yogurt is completely submerged in the water and it forms a thin gelatin skin. Slide 7 or 8 spoonfuls of yogurt into the water at a time, being careful not to let the balls touch each other. Allow the balls to sit in the alginated water for 2 minutes to set the surrounding skin. Then, using a slotted spoon, gently transfer the balls to another baking dish filled with the remaining 2 cups of mineral water. Let the balls soak in the water for 30 seconds. Using the slotted spoon, transfer the balls to the serving plate. Repeat the process with the remaining mixture. You should have at least 24 yogurt balls.

Peel 5 of the clementines. Remove the clementine segments by slicing toward the core on each side of the membranes. Slice the segments in half lengthwise and set in a mixing bowl. Grate the zest from the remaining clementine with a microplane and add to the mixing bowl. Juice the clementine and add the juice to the mixing bowl. Stir in the honey and the sweet wine.

To serve, gently transfer 6 yogurt balls to each of 4 dessert plates. Spoon the clementine mixture around the yogurt balls and garnish with mint leaves.

We often talk about avant-garde cooking versus home cooking, but we need to remember that what we think of as traditional cooking was, not so long ago, considered modern cooking. This brings out the magic of every ingredient, though it requires a few special items you may have to seek out on the Internet or in specialty stores. The goal is to convert water into a little ball that is still liquid inside. It's no surprise that this technique is from El Bulli, where Ferran Adrià is changing the restaurant world with his innovations.

Higos en Malvasía

Figs in sweet Malvasía wine

SERVES 4

2 CUPS SWEET SPANISH MALVASÍA WINE OR A GOOD-QUALITY MUSCAT

1¼ TEASPOONS UNFLAVORED GELATIN POWDER

2 ORANGES

4 RIPE BUT FIRM BLACK MISSION FIGS

¼ CUP FRESH MINT LEAVES

ZEST OF 1 LEMON

Warm ½ cup of the wine in a small pot over low heat, then add the gelatin and let it dissolve in the wine. Do not let the wine boil. Stir in the remaining 1½ cups of wine. Pour the wine into 4 large shallow soup bowls and refrigerate for 30 minutes or until a gelée forms on the bottom of the bowl.

Meanwhile, zest both oranges and set the zest aside. Slice off the top and bottom of each orange. Using a sharp knife, cut down the sides of the oranges to remove all of the peel and pith. Slice along the sides of each membrane and pull out the segments.

Cut the figs into quarters. Arrange the fig quarters on top of the wine gelée. Arrange the orange segments on top of the figs and garnish with the mint leaves and lemon and orange zests.

When you travel around Spain, you see fig trees in the middle of the countryside with big open leaves like enormous hands trying to grab the sky. Figs are indigenous to Spain, and when they're in season, the markets are full of them. Sometimes they are so ripe that a mere touch breaks them open. This dish celebrates that sweetness and ripeness.

Arroz con leche

Rice and milk dessert

SERVES 4

5 CUPS WHOLE MILK

1 CUP HEAVY CREAM

½ VANILLA BEAN

1 CINNAMON STICK

½ CUP SPANISH BOMBA OR CALASPARRA RICE

2 TABLESPOONS UNSALTED BUTTER

1 CUP SUGAR

Pour the milk and cream into a large pot, add the vanilla bean and cinnamon stick, and bring to a boil over high heat. Once the milk boils, remove the cinnamon stick and vanilla bean. Add the rice, reduce the heat to low, and simmer for 40 minutes. Keep stirring with a wooden spoon to prevent the rice from sticking to the bottom of the pot.

Remove the rice from the heat and stir in the butter, little by little, until it has melted into the rice. Add the sugar and mix in well. Let the rice rest for 3 to 4 hours, or until completely cooled.

Just before serving, stir the rice, folding in the thin skin that has formed on the top. Divide the rice pudding among 4 dessert bowls and serve at room temperature.

José's Tip:

If you like, you can sprinkle 2 tablespoons sugar over the top of the rice pudding and brown it with a kitchen torch. Hold the torch about 2 inches away from the sugared surface of the rice and heat until the sugar is deep brown and forms a crust.

This is from the great restaurant Casa Gerardo, where my friend Pedro Morán and his family produce some of the best food in Spain. It's the perfect place to taste traditional and creative dishes at the same time. I wish there were more places like this, where tradition and modernity go hand in hand.

Churros

Sweet fried Dough

SERVES 4

½ CUP UNSALTED BUTTER

¼ TEASPOON SEA SALT

2 CUPS ALL-PURPOSE FLOUR

3 LARGE EGGS

4 CUPS SPANISH EXTRA-VIRGIN OLIVE OIL

¼ CUP SUGAR

2 CUPS SPANISH HOT CHOCOLATE (PAGE 237)

Combine the butter, salt, and 2 cups of water in a medium pot. Heat over medium-low heat until the mixture begins to boil, then stir in the flour. Reduce the heat to low and stir vigorously until the batter forms a ball. Remove the pot from the heat.

Beat the eggs in a mixing bowl until smooth. Gradually stir the eggs into the batter until well combined. Spoon the batter into a pastry bag fitted with a star tip, then fold down the sides of the bag to compress the batter.

Heat the olive oil in a large pot until it measures 350°F on a candy thermometer. Squeeze 3 or 4 4-inch strips of batter into the hot oil. Fry, turning the strips, until golden brown, about 4 minutes. Transfer the churros to a paper towel–lined plate to drain. Spread the sugar on a plate. While the churros are still hot, roll them in the sugar. Repeat with the remaining batter, allowing the oil to return to 350°F between batches. Serve the churros with small cups of hot chocolate.

Churros are more than just crunchy strips of sweet fried dough: They are a breakfast institution in Spain. Dipped into a cup of thick hot chocolate, they are the perfect start to the day—or, as is often the case on a Spanish weekend, the perfect end to a long night.

castilla la mancha

When I was a kid, my imagination was a landscape filled with superheroes fighting intergalactic battles and conquering planets. Castilla La Mancha has been that kind of place (though the battles were over castles, not planets) since the days of Don Quixote. Cervantes's great seventeenth-century novel tells the story of a delusional old man's quest to become a hero to damsels in distress and others who need his help. He's a fascinating character, but even more extraordinary is his servant and sidekick, Sancho Panza, whose only mission is to make sure his master doesn't get into trouble. Of course, for me, the interesting moments in this masterpiece are the references to food and eating. Cervantes's obsession with food reflects an otherwise little-known Spanish gastronomic legacy in this period.

Reading *Don Quixote* reveals Spain's incredible culinary depth over the last five hundred years. Today you can find restaurants in Castilla La Mancha that offer whole menus based on the simple food that features in Cervantes's book. And you can still visit the windmills that figure so prominently in his work. The first time I saw them, I looked at them with the eyes of a child. They made me think of all the wheat milled by those ancient winds of La Mancha, the smells of the bread baking, and the food that was served next to that beautiful fresh bread.

I am still in awe of the extraordinary food produced in this region. Here you'll find Las Pedroñeras, the garlic capital of Spain, with its magical purple garlic that is both sweet and strong. The world-famous Manchego cheese is made from the region's sheep's milk, and there's sweet honey from Alcarria and smooth marzipan from Toledo.

But the real culinary magic of this region rises from the earth each fall, when the small, mauve *Crocus sativus* emerges. For months, the fields look like nothing more than a mess of mud and stones. Then one day, the flowers emerge. Inside are the delicate stigmas known the world over as saffron. Picking begins immediately, before the petals have a chance to open in the sun. Lightly toasted and sealed in an airtight container, this precious seasoning releases its special aroma and deep color only when infused into paella, stews, soups, and even desserts. It may sound as extraordinary as one of Don Quixote's flights of fancy, but it is as real as the fields of La Mancha.

1800
AZAFRAN
PRINCESA
MINAYA

Nobody knows where or when vines first grew in Spain, but most Spanish wine-lovers guess we have the Phoenicians to thank for their work, around 3,000 years ago. They founded the cities of Cadíz and Jerez, and the latter gave its name to a special form of winemaking in Spain: sherry. By the late Roman period, Spanish wine was one of the most widely traded products in the Mediterranean region. Under Muslim rule, winemaking continued, even though drinking was prohibited under the Koran. After the Reconquest, wines developed further in Spain's monasteries and beyond. The greatest impact on Spanish wines, though, was the devastation the phylloxera pest wreaked on the vineyards of France. Many French winemakers survived by transplanting their grapes and their winemaking techniques to La Rioja and Ribera del Duero, two great Spanish wine regions. Today, Spain has devoted more land to vines than any other country in the world, including France, Italy, and the United States.

Drinks in Spain extend well beyond its many wonderful wines. Spaniards love nothing better than a great cocktail, and I believe we make the best gin and tonics in the world—no matter what my English friends say. As in all Spanish cuisine, the factors that make our cocktails surpass all the others are the quality and freshness of our ingredients.

drinks

LA RIOJA
DAVALILLO
DAVALILLO
RIOJA
DAVALILLO
DAVALILLO
VINOS
Pimiento de "CALAHORR
VIÑA ZACO
HARO
MARCA CONCEDIDA
La Rioja Al
SOCIEDAD DE COSECHEROS DE V
FUNDADA EN 1890
Haro
VIÑA ARDANZA

la rioja

My first contact with wine came at a young age in Barcelona. One of the snacks we would eat just before lunch or a couple of hours before dinner was a piece of toasted bread sprinkled with drops of red wine and a spoonful of sugar. More often than not, we would want seconds or thirds (even if we rarely got them).

At that time, thirty years ago, most wine was simply referred to generically as *white* or *red*. When someone wanted to suggest a wine was especially good, he would put the words *La Rioja* in front of it. La Rioja was one of the first regions in Spain to establish a controlled production area, or D.O., which means not a single drop of wine leaves the region unbottled. It's a guarantee of the wine's quality as well as an indication of the sophistication of the wine region in La Rioja.

The name *Rioja* comes from the river Rio Oja, one of the seven sources of the great Ebro River. Wines were produced here in the days of the Phoenicians, and they were formally recognized in the Middle Ages by the king of nearby Navarre and Aragón. The Ebro River is flanked by fertile plains where farmers grow wonderful fruit and vegetables. The cauliflowers of Calahorra are so special that they too are officially regulated, with their own D.O. These cauliflowers will turn any carnivore into a vegetable lover with their profound flavor and texture. Small wonder that one of the most famous dishes here is menestra, a mix of cauliflower, artichokes, green beans, chard, peas, and carrots. Throw in a little ham and olive oil, and you have one of the best vegetable dishes in the world.

Sangría Tinto

Red wine sangría

SERVES 4

1 BOTTLE OF FRUITY RED WINE, SUCH AS A GARNACHA

5 TABLESPOONS BRANDY

¼ CUP COINTREAU OR OTHER TOP-QUALITY ORANGE-FLAVORED LIQUEUR

¼ CUP VODKA

1 SPLASH RUBY PORT

1 ORANGE, PEELED AND SLICED

2 GRANNY SMITH APPLES, CORED AND DICED

1 CINNAMON STICK

1 STRIP OF LEMON ZEST

¼ CUP FRESH ORANGE JUICE

1 SPLASH OF SODA WATER

Combine the wine, brandy, Cointreau, vodka, port, orange, apples, cinnamon stick, and lemon zest in a bowl and refrigerate for at least 4 hours. Pour the mixture into a pitcher filled halfway with ice. Add the orange juice and soda water, give a quick stir, and serve. Make sure each glass gets some ice and fruit.

This is one of the most popular drinks in my Jaleo restaurants. Find out for yourself just how good it is.

Sangría Blanca

White wine sangría

SERVES 4

- 1 CUP CHOPPED MIXED FRESH FRUIT, SUCH AS STRAWBERRIES, PEACHES, AND WHITE GRAPES
- 1 BOTTLE OF CAVA (SPANISH DRY SPARKLING WINE)
- ¼ CUP BRANDY
- ¼ CUP LICOR 43 OR OTHER VANILLA-FLAVORED LIQUEUR
- ¼ CUP WHITE GRAPE JUICE
- 1 TEASPOON SUGAR
- 1 SMALL FRESH MINT SPRIG

Fill a glass pitcher halfway with ice and add the chopped fruit. Tilt the pitcher and pour the cava very slowly down the side; this will help retain the bubbles. In another pitcher, combine the brandy, Licor 43, white grape juice, and sugar, then pour the mixture into the sparkling wine and fruit. Give a quick stir and add the mint sprig. When serving, make sure each glass gets some ice and fruit.

The white version of our great Jaleo sangría. Use fruits in season when making this refreshing version.

Sangre Gazpacho

Gazpacho Bloody Mary

SERVES 4

- 8 CHERRY TOMATOES
- ½ TEASPOON FRESHLY GRATED HORSERADISH
- ¼ TEASPOON CELERY SEEDS
- ⅛ TEASPOON COARSELY GROUND BLACK PEPPER
- ¼ TEASPOON CAYENNE
- 2½ TABLESPOONS WORCESTERSHIRE SAUCE
- 4 CUPS GAZPACHO (PAGE 43)
- ½ CUP ABSOLUT CITRON OR OTHER TOP-QUALITY LEMON-FLAVORED VODKA
- 4 ROMAINE LETTUCE LEAVES (TENDER INNER LEAVES ONLY)

Slide 2 cherry tomatoes onto each of 4 6-inch wooden skewers and set aside.

Mix the horseradish, celery seeds, black pepper, cayenne, and Worcestershire sauce together in a pitcher. Pour the gazpacho and the vodka into the pitcher and stir well. Serve in highball glasses, garnished with the romaine leaves and cherry tomato skewers.

A uniquely Spanish and refreshing take on a familiar cocktail.

Horchata

Tiger nut milk

SERVES 4

2 CUPS CHUFA NUTS (TIGER NUTS)

½ CINNAMON STICK

1 TEASPOON GRATED LEMON ZEST

½ CUP SUGAR

1 QUART FLAT MINERAL OR FILTERED WATER

Soak the tiger nuts in water for 24 hours. Drain the nuts and place them in a blender with the cinnamon stick, lemon zest, and sugar. Add the water and blend until smooth. Line a fine-mesh strainer with cheesecloth and strain the mixture into a bowl. Squeeze the cheesecloth to release as much liquid as possible. Discard the solids and chill the milk. Stir well before pouring into cups. Serve cold.

Horchata is a refreshing summer drink popular in Valencia, where the tiger nuts grow. While sweet and nutty in flavor, the tiger nut is actually a tuber, first planted in Spain by the Arabs.

José's Tip:
Tiger nuts, or chufa nuts, can be found in health food stores and Latin markets.

Queimada

Galician punch

SERVES 4

4 OUNCES SPANISH ORUJO (GALICIAN CLEAR DISTILLED SPIRIT) OR OTHER HIGH-ALCOHOL CLEAR LIQUOR, SUCH AS GRAPPA OR PISCO

6 TABLESPOONS SUGAR

1 STRIP LEMON ZEST

8–10 COFFEE BEANS (OPTIONAL)

6–8 APPLE OR ORANGE SLICES (OPTIONAL)

Pour the alcohol into a small pot and stir in the sugar and lemon zest. Cook the mixture over medium-high heat, stirring with a wooden spoon, until the sugar dissolves, about 3 minutes. Once the sugar melts, carefully light the alcohol with a match. When the flame turns blue, extinguish the flame by covering the pot with a lid and removing it from the stove. Drop in some coffee beans and slices of fruit, if you like. Queimada is traditionally served warm in clay cups.

Drinking this punch in Galicia was one of the highlights of making *Made in Spain*, especially because it's supposed to be drunk after saying a special prayer or magic spell. Make it yourself and cast your own spell.

Fuerte y dulce martini

Sweet martini

SERVES 4

½ CUP SUGAR

¾ CUP HENDRICK'S GIN OR OTHER TOP-QUALITY GIN

¼ CUP LATE-HARVEST MONASTRELL WINE (SEE TIP)

¼ CUP FRESH LEMON JUICE

4 LEMON TWISTS (OPTIONAL)

José's Tip:
Monastrell is sweet, dark, ruby-colored wine from the warm regions of Spain. It is similar to Mourvèdre.

Prepare a simple syrup by putting the sugar in a small saucepan with ½ cup water. Stir over medium-high heat until the sugar dissolves, about 10 minutes. Remove from the heat and let the syrup cool in the refrigerator.

Pour the gin, Monastrell, lemon juice, and ¼ cup of the simple syrup into a pitcher and stir. Put 1 cup of ice into a metal shaker, pour in one-quarter of the liquid, cover, and shake. Strain the liquid into a chilled martini glass and garnish with a lemon twist, if you like. Repeat to make 3 more cocktails.

The best martini you'll ever taste—sweet and strong.

Cremat

Burnt rum

SERVES 4

8 COFFEE BEANS

1 STRIP OF LEMON ZEST

1 TABLESPOON FRESH LEMON JUICE

1 SHOT OF ESPRESSO

8 TEASPOONS SUGAR

2 CINNAMON STICKS

2 CUPS DARK RUM

Mix the coffee beans, lemon zest, lemon juice, espresso, 4 teaspoons of the sugar, the cinnamon sticks, and 1½ cups of the rum together in a small pot. Pour the remaining ½ cup of rum into another small pot. Carefully ignite the ½ cup rum with a match, then slowly pour the burning rum into the coffee-rum mixture. Carefully stir the liquid with the bottom of a ladle to mix the ingredients well. Sprinkle the remaining 4 teaspoons of sugar over the burning mixture and stir until the flame subsides. Serve in clay cups.

Cremat is best enjoyed on the Costa Brava, the beautiful coastline of Catalonia, while singing a habanera song. These songs were brought to Spain by the Catalans, who fought alongside the Cubans in the Cuban-American war. They also carried back the rum that makes this drink. Sometimes a war's influences aren't all bad.

Limonada de Manzanilla

Sherry lemonade

SERVES 4

3 LEMONS, CUT INTO QUARTERS

4 TABLESPOONS SUGAR

2 CUPS SPANISH MANZANILLA SHERRY

2 TABLESPOONS TRIPLE SEC

SODA WATER

Combine 3 of the lemon wedges with 1 tablespoon of the sugar in a pint glass and muddle using a pestle or wooden spoon. Add 1 cup of ice, ½ cup of sherry, and 1½ teaspoons triple sec. Cover the pint glass with the bottom half of a metal shaker and shake vigorously for 30 seconds. Pour into a highball glass and top with a splash of soda water. Make 3 more cocktails in the same way.

A hard lemonade from my favorite part of Andalusia—sherry country.

Sol de Limón

Lemon Sun

SERVES 4

1 CUP MIGUEL TORRES OR OTHER TOP-QUALITY SPANISH BRANDY

¾ CUP LICOR 43 OR OTHER VANILLA-FLAVORED LIQUEUR

¾ CUP FRESH LEMON JUICE

4 STRIPS LEMON ZEST (FROM THE LEMONS USED FOR JUICE)

Fill a metal shaker with 1 cup of ice, and then add half of the brandy, half of the liqueur, and half of the lemon juice. Shake vigorously for 30 seconds. Pour into 2 8-ounce rocks glasses and garnish with a twist of lemon. Repeat for the second batch.

A refreshingly lemony cocktail that also packs a punch.

Mimosa de cava con aire de clementina

Cava mimosa with clementine air

SERVES 4

1 CLEMENTINE

¼ TEASPOON LECITHIN

1 CUP FRESH CLEMENTINE JUICE (FROM ABOUT 6 CLEMENTINES)

1 BOTTLE OF CAVA (SPANISH SPARKLING WINE)

Peel the clementine, reserving the peel, and remove the segments by slicing toward the core on each side of the membranes with a sharp knife. Pull out the segments and set aside.

Combine the lecithin and clementine juice in a mixing bowl. Cover the bowl tightly with plastic wrap, then make a small hole in the center of the plastic wrap and insert an immersion blender. Tilt the bowl slightly to the side and, with the blender positioned just on the top of the liquid, mix on high speed until you have a frothy foam. Be sure to dissolve all of the lecithin. The froth should form stiff peaks that will hold for about 30 minutes. (You can mix again with the blender if it deflates.)

Rub the rims of 4 champagne glasses with the clementine peel, then pour in the cava. Top each glass with a large spoonful of clementine air and garnish with a segment of clementine.

José's Tip:
Lecithin is a natural emulsifier and food supplement. It can be found in health food stores and online. I recommend the Texturas brand from my friend Ferran Adrià.

In Madrid and Barcelona, the influence of the American cocktail is strong. During the 1930s and 1940s, cocktail bars specializing in American-style drinks were common and popular. Some of them, like Boadas in Barcelona, have become landmarks in their own right. This drink contains cava, the sparkling wine made in Catalonia.

Chocolate a la taza

Spanish hot chocolate

SERVES 4

4½ CUPS WHOLE MILK

10½ OUNCES BITTERSWEET CHOCOLATE (PREFERABLY 70% COCOA), BROKEN INTO SMALL PIECES

1 TABLESPOON SUGAR

1 TEASPOON GROUND CINNAMON

Combine the milk, chocolate, and sugar in a medium saucepan. Whisk the milk mixture vigorously over high heat until the chocolate and sugar dissolve, about 10 minutes; do not let it boil. Pour the thick liquid into mugs and garnish with a sprinkle of cinnamon.

Europe needs to thank Spain for chocolate, since it was Spanish explorers who brought the magical food back from the New World, and it was a Spanish king—Charles V—who popularized it. So try our version of hot chocolate and become a king or queen for a day.

Ginebra con tónica

Gin and tonic

SERVES 2

4 OUNCES HENDRICK'S GIN OR OTHER TOP-QUALITY GIN, PLUS A BIT MORE

4 OUNCES TOP-QUALITY TONIC WATER OR MORE TO TASTE (SEE TIP)

2 STRIPS LEMON ZEST

1 TEASPOON DRIED JUNIPER BERRIES

Fill 2 8-ounce rocks glasses three-quarters full of ice. Pour 2 ounces of gin over the ice in each glass. Top each with about 2 ounces of tonic water. Twist the peel over the ice to release its oils, then rub the rim with the peel and drop it into the glass. Drop in a few juniper berries and, holding your thumb over the opening of the gin bottle, float a tiny layer of gin on top.

It is a well-known fact that I make the best gin and tonics in the world. Aromatic with lemon and juniper, they are inspired by the wonderful gin and tonics I sampled in the Balearic Islands, where they make an amazing gin as the result of years of British occupation.

José's Tip:
Never use big bottles of tonic—they go flat too fast. Always get the small (6- to 8-ounce) bottles and open a fresh one every time you make a cocktail. Melting ice is also your enemy; it will dilute the cocktail. Use large cubes right out of the freezer!

baleares

The first summer vacation I can remember was to Mallorca, the largest of the Balearic Islands, with my whole family, all of us excited and happy to cross the Mediterranean. There I encountered the most incredible pastries, like the spiraled ensaimada, whose light texture—somewhere between a croissant and puff pastry—is due to the pork fat it contains. Today I can't see an ensaimada without buying one, even if I take only a single bite.

Those pastries weren't the only surprising food on the island. Each day for breakfast we ate sobrasada, a buttery sausage with pimentón that has an extraordinary texture. It is more of a paste than a traditional sausage, and you spread it on toasted bread or sear it lightly on a griddle. Sobrasada is made from the Mallorcan black pig (not to be confused with the Ibérico black pig, used to produce Spain's best hams), mixed with different combinations of herbs. The unique flavor is the result of the damp climate on the islands, where meat can't be cured by air-drying as it is on the mainland. Instead, pimentón is added as a preservative, which gives the sausage its distinctive color and flavor. All across the island you will see sobrasada hanging from the ceilings of stores and homes.

What really stood out for me on Mallorca was probably the most humble food produced on these islands. Right in the heart of Mallorca is a town called Inca where they make a very special bread—a tiny 1-inch-thick loaf that is as hard as a rock. Nothing represents the spirit of the islanders quite as well as that tough, simple bread from Inca.

On the other Balearic island of Menorca is more wonderful gastronomic history. There they produce Mahón cheese, its slightly salty tang due to the island's pastures, which are infused with the flavors of the sea air. The town of Mahón itself was occupied several times by the British, who popularized two great products: mayonnaise, from Mahón, and the town's favorite spirit, gin. Forget what you know about dull, lifeless gin and tonics. The best gin and tonics are those made in Spain, with plenty of lemon and ice.

33

The sauces of Spain are as varied as our regions. They can serve as stand-alone creations, so rich and flavorful in their own right that they dominate a dish, or they can be the foundation of something bigger, like a complex paella or hearty stew.

Consider the sauces of my home region of Catalonia. Much of our cooking involves one of four essential sauces: allioli (a garlic and olive oil emulsion), picada (a thick paste of almonds, hazelnuts, and/or pinenuts combined with garlic, parsley, and sometimes fried bread used to thicken stews), sofregit (caramelized onion and tomato called sofrito in Spanish), and samfaina (a sofrito with eggplant and zucchini).

Even as a chef who grew up in Catalonia, I have to pay my respects to the great sauces used throughout the Canaries. The mojo sauces from the islands accompany fish, meats and vegetable dishes. There are two basic versions: mojo rojo, a red sauce that is either spicy or sweet, and mojo verde, a green sauce, usually made with parsley or cilantro. Fresh and versatile, they represent a strong gastronomic link between the old and new worlds, mixing European garlic and olive oil with the American peppers and herbs that revolutionized Spanish cooking. You will find numerous uses for all these sauces in your everyday cooking once you add them to your repertoire.

sau

MAXORATA

canarias

The Canary Islands are a geographic and gastronomic link between Europe, Africa, and Latin America. Since the times of Christopher Columbus, they were always the last port of call for European sailors on their way to the New World because they were close to the ocean currents that carried boats all the way to America.

Columbus noticed many similarities between the Canaries and the Caribbean islands he had just discovered. So, on his second voyage to the Caribbean, he took sugarcane from the Canaries, as well as livestock and seeds. Bananas went to the future Dominican Republic, black pigs went to Cuba, and gofio grain went to Puerto Rico.

In spite of this wonderful history, the people of the Canaries have always felt forgotten by the rest of Spain, not unlike Hawaii's feeling about the continental United States. They are part of the country, but they're also at a distance. While this is considered a bad thing by many locals, it also explains why the Canary Islands are among the most distinctive places in Spain—and the whole of Europe.

The culture of the Canaries is strikingly different from that of most other regions of Spain. The local accent is such a beautiful mix of Castilian and Latin American that you can't help but fall in love with a person speaking it. The islanders celebrate carnival as enthusiastically as the Brazilians do in Rio de Janeiro, and the food is a hybrid of various regions of Spain, Latin America, and the Caribbean. The islanders use eggplant as much as they use yucca or corn. Their traditional sauce is a mojo picada, which resembles a sauce from Mexico. They love their potatoes, which they call *papas,* as in Latin America. They grill the distinctive local fish over the lava from the island's volcano. It's hard to find another place where the people are so united with their environment. Even the grapes are special; the vines in Lanzarote go deep into the ground to pull the moisture out of the dark volcanic earth. The result is a wonderfully sweet wine with an extraordinary history. Today they call it Malvasía, but its old name was Canary, and it was one of Thomas Jefferson's favorite wines. In that sense, it was the original taste of Spain in the Americas.

Mojo verde

Canary Island green pepper sauce

MAKES 1½ CUPS

- 3 GARLIC CLOVES, PEELED
- ½ TEASPOON SEA SALT
- 1 CUP WELL-PACKED CHOPPED CILANTRO LEAVES
- ¼ TEASPOON CUMIN SEEDS
- ¼ CUP SPANISH EXTRA-VIRGIN OLIVE OIL
- 1 TEASPOON SHERRY VINEGAR

Using a mortar and pestle, mash the garlic and salt together until you have a smooth paste. Rotate the mortar while you mash, scraping down the garlic from the sides with the pestle. Add the cilantro and cumin and keep mashing until the ingredients are well combined. Slowly drizzle in the olive oil as you continue to mash the paste, making sure the olive oil is absorbed. Drizzle in 1 teaspoon of water and the vinegar. Turn the pestle with a slow, continuous circular motion around the mortar as you drizzle the liquids into the sauce. Keep the sauce at room temperature until ready to use.

José's Tip:
Fresh parsley can also be used to make this sauce.

Mojo rojo

Canary Island red pepper sauce

MAKES 1½ CUPS

- 6 GARLIC CLOVES, PEELED
- ½ TEASPOON SEA SALT
- ½ TEASPOON CUMIN SEEDS
- 1 TEASPOON SWEET PIMENTÓN (SPANISH SMOKED PAPRIKA)
- 1 DRIED GUINDILLA PEPPER (OR YOUR FAVORITE DRIED CHILE PEPPER)
- ¼ CUP SPANISH EXTRA-VIRGIN OLIVE OIL
- 1 TEASPOON SHERRY VINEGAR

Using a mortar and pestle, mash the garlic and salt to a smooth paste. Rotate the mortar as you mash, scraping down the garlic from the sides with the pestle. Add the cumin, pimentón, and chile pepper and keep mashing until the ingredients are well combined. Slowly drizzle in the olive oil as you continue to mash the paste, making sure the olive oil is absorbed. Drizzle in 1 teaspoon water and the vinegar. Turn the pestle with a slow, continuous circular motion around the mortar as you drizzle the liquids into the sauce. Keep the sauce at room temperature until ready to use.

José's Tip:
For uncooked sauces using garlic, it's important to use very fresh garlic cloves. Stale cloves are more pungent and bitter.

Sofrito

Catalan tomato and onion sauce

MAKES 3 CUPS

- 10 RIPE PLUM TOMATOES
- 1½ CUPS SPANISH EXTRA-VIRGIN OLIVE OIL
- 4 SMALL SPANISH ONIONS, FINELY CHOPPED (ABOUT 4 CUPS)
- 1 TEASPOON SUGAR
- 1 TEASPOON SALT
- 1 TEASPOON SWEET PIMENTÓN (SPANISH SMOKED PAPRIKA)
- 3 BAY LEAVES

Slice the tomatoes in half. Place a grater over a mixing bowl. Rub the cut surface of the tomatoes over the grater until all of the flesh is grated. Discard the skins.

Heat the oil in a medium saucepan over medium-low heat. Add the onions, sugar, and salt. Cook, stirring occasionally, until the onions are soft and golden brown, about 45 minutes. You want the onions to caramelize; if they get too dark, add ½ teaspoon of water to keep them from burning.

Stir in the tomato purée, the pimentón, and the bay leaves and cook for another 20 minutes over medium heat. You'll know the sofrito is ready when the tomato has broken down and deepened in color and the oil has separated from the sauce. Discard the bay leaves.

José's Tip:
This sauce is used in many, many recipes. Store it in the refrigerator, covered, for up to 5 days.

Salmorra

Smoky tomato and garlic sauce

MAKES 2 CUPS

1 TABLESPOON SPANISH EXTRA-VIRGIN OLIVE OIL

12 GARLIC CLOVES, PEELED

3 ÑORA CHILE PEPPERS (OR ANY OTHER DRIED SWEET CHILE PEPPER), SEEDED

16 OUNCES CANNED PLUM TOMATOES, DRAINED

1 TEASPOON SUGAR

⅛ TEASPOON SWEET PIMENTÓN (SPANISH SMOKED PAPRIKA)

SALT TO TASTE

Heat the oil in a medium pot over medium heat. Add the garlic and sauté until soft, about 2 minutes. Add the chile peppers and toast, stirring, for about 3 minutes, then add the tomatoes and sugar. Cook for 15 minutes or until the tomato liquid evaporates. Stir in the pimentón. Transfer the mixture to a blender and purée. Pour into a bowl and season to taste with salt.

José's Tip:
This sauce can be kept in the refrigerator, covered, for up to 2 weeks or frozen for up to 3 months. Be sure to drizzle the top of the sauce with olive oil before you cover it to prevent it from drying out.

Allioli

Garlic mayonnaise

MAKES ABOUT 1 CUP

4 GARLIC CLOVES, PEELED

PINCH OF SEA SALT

½ TEASPOON FRESH LEMON JUICE (FROM ABOUT ¼ LEMON)

1½ CUPS SPANISH EXTRA-VIRGIN OLIVE OIL

Using a mortar and pestle, mash the garlic and salt together until you have a smooth paste. Turn the mortar while you mash, scraping down the garlic from the sides with the pestle. Add the lemon juice and then add the olive oil, drop by drop, as you continue to crush the paste with the pestle. Keep turning the pestle with a slow, continuous circular motion around the mortar as you drip the oil in slowly and steadily, making sure the paste absorbs the olive oil. Keep adding the oil until the sauce has the consistency of a very thick mayonnaise. If your allioli becomes too dense, add ½ teaspoon of water to thin it. This process takes time—around 20 minutes of slow, circular motions around the mortar—to create a dense, rich sauce.

José's Tip:
If you're short on time, use a hand-held electric mixer, adding the oil little by little as you blend at high speed. Be sure to use the freshest garlic available.

Agradecimientos

acknowledgments

Anyone who creates a televison series *and* a cookbook truly understands the meaning of team effort. *Made in Spain* is the product of an amazing team, and there are many people I need to thank for their help in the realization of this work. If I tried to name everyone who was involved with this project, I'm sure I would leave someone out, so my heartfelt thanks go to you all. You know who you are. You know your contribution. I am proud of you, and I hope you are very proud of what we accomplished together.

I want to thank the team at THINKfoodGROUP, especially Ann McCarthy, Ruben Garcia, and JohnPaul Damato who helped with the conception, research, organization, development, recipe testing, filming, and photographing of this project. You are the best. Thank you for your support during what has been the busiest phase of my life—so far.

Thanks to Thomas Schauer, whose beautiful photographs of the recipes helped to bring this cookbook to life. Thanks also to Roberto Sablayrolles of Tasty Concepts for his innovative designs.

Thanks to everyone at Clarkson Potter, especially Pam Krauss, for believing in us and adapting with us on this journey. And thanks to Kris Dahl at ICM for always fighting in our corner.

Thanks to Full Plate Media, Philip Lerman, and the television crews in the United States and in Spain who helped make my show a reality. Thanks to KQED for supporting the show and to PBS for giving it a home.

Thanks to the Instituto Español de Comercio Exterior (ICEX), its Foods from Spain and Wines from Spain teams, and the Instituto de Turismo de España (Turespaña) for their continued support. Thanks to all our friends listed in Resources (opposite) for showing how private businesses can help sell the best of Spain to the world. And thanks to all the farmers and fishermen, chefs and bakers, artisans and ham makers who have helped make Spain one of the most amazing destinations in the world.

Finally, thanks to my friend and coauthor Richard Wolffe for helping me give voice to the thoughts in my head and my heart.

José Andrés
Washington, D.C.

resources

Many of the recipes from *Made in Spain* call for authentic Spanish products. Trust me: It is worth the time it takes to seek them out. Just a few years ago, finding products from Spain would have been a challenge, but today my country's cheeses, sausages, hams, and more are widely available. Supermarkets across the country like Whole Foods or Wegmans—as well as specialty retailers like Balducci's, Dean & DeLuca, and Trader Joe's—are stocking more and more Spanish products. If you can't find what you need at your local shops, be sure to ask for it or check out one of our favorite resources below.

Cowgirl Creamery
Award-winning cheesemakers in their own right, this shop also imports beautiful artisan cheeses from Spain and other parts of Europe. Retail outlets can be found in San Francisco and Washington, D.C.
www.cowgirlcreamery.com

Despaña
For more than thirty-five years, this company has been bringing the flavors of Spain to America, including their own house-made chorizo and morcilla sausages. Recently, they opened a retail boutique in New York City.
www.despanabrandfoods.com

La Española Meats
This California-based company has long been considered a pioneer in the importing of Spanish products. And although they offer Spanish rice, oils, and peppers, it is their Spanish-style sausages and cured meats that have garnered them recognition.
www.laespanolameats.com

La Tienda
Located in Williamsburg, Virginia, this is your one-stop shop for all things Spanish. The Harris family searches across Spain for the most authentic products and delivers them right to your door through their website and catalog.
www.tienda.com

The Spanish Table
From olive oil and sherry vinegar to preserved tuna and white asparagus, this outlet has a wide selection of food stuffs, cookbooks, and tableware—even paella pans to serve two hundred! You can visit their stores in Seattle, Santa Fe, Berkeley, and Mill Valley, California.
www.spanishtable.com

Zingerman's
A well-known purveyor of fine foods, this Ann Arbor, Michigan, company has a growing assortment of products from Spain, including cheeses, spices, and almonds.
www.zingermans.com

index

Note: *Italicized* page numbers refer to recipe photographs.